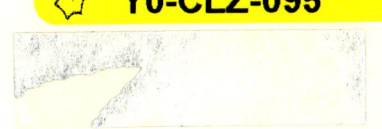

8058796

Lit 170 B666p
Bodenheimer, Edgar, 1908-
Philosophy of responsibility
/
$18.50

**DISCARDED BY
MEMPHIS PUBLIC LIBRARY**

MAIN LIBRARY

Memphis and Shelby
County Public Library and
Information Center

For the Residents
of
Memphis and Shelby County

PHILOSOPHY OF RESPONSIBILITY

PHILOSOPHY OF RESPONSIBILITY

Edgar Bodenheimer

FRED B. ROTHMAN & CO.
Littleton, Colorado   80123
1980

Library of Congress Cataloging in Publication Data

BODENHEIMER, EDGAR, (date)
　Philosophy of Responsibility.

　　Includes bibliographical references and index.
　　1.—Responsibility. I.—Title.
BJ1451.B6　　　170　　　　　　　79-26020
ISBN 0-8377-0309-5

© 1980 by Edgar Bodenheimer
All rights reserved.

Printed in the U.S.A.

To my wife Brigitte
 who gave inestimable help and counsel

Table of Contents
―――――――――――

Preface   ix

Introductory Statement   1

PART I: A GENERAL THEORY OF RESPONSIBILITY

Chapter 1: *The Meaning and Roots of Responsibility*   5
    A. The Meaning of Responsibility   5
    B. Responsibility and Blameworthiness   9
    C. The Roots of Responsibility   10

Chapter 2: *Responsibility and Freewill*   14
    A. The Relevance of Freewill   14
    B. Causal Laws and Causal Occurences   17
    C. Causes and Reasons   22
    D. The Battle of Motives   23
    E. The Indelible Character   26
    F. The Modern Synthesis   27

Chapter 3: *The Limits of Responsibility*   30
    A. Introductory Observations   30
    B. Voluntary and Involuntary Acts   31
    C. The Reality of Mental Disease   34
    D. Proposals to Abolish the Insanity Defense   37
    E. The Legal Tests of Insanity   41
    F. Diminished Responsibility   45
    G. Conclusion   49

PART II: THE VARIETIES OF RESPONSIBILITY

Chapter 4: *Existential Responsibility*   53
- A. Foundations of Existential Responsibility   53
- B. Responsibility and Common Human Traits   54
- C. Responsibility and Individual Traits   57
- D. Responsibility for Self-Perfection   60
- E. Egotism and Altruism   63

Chapter 5: *Responsibility in Sexual and Family Relationships*   67
- A. Responsibility Toward Sexual Partners   67
- B. Responsibility Toward Spouses   72
- C. Responsibility Toward Children   74
- D. Responsibility Toward Parents   82

Chapter 6: *Responsibility Toward Fellow Human Beings*   86
- A. Preliminary Observations   86
- B. Principled and Individualized Morality   88
- C. Situation Ethics   90
- D. Universal Ethical Principles   94
- E. Conflicts between Ethical Values   96
- F. Relations between Moral and Legal Responsibility   97

Chapter 7: *Social and Political Responsibility*   102
- A. Social Responsibility   102
- B. Social Responsibility and Self-Interest   105
- C. Conflicts between Moral and Social Responsibility   107
- D. Political Responsibility   107
- E. Human Rights and Civic Obligations   110
- F. Power and Responsibility   112
- G. Anonymity of Responsibility   117

Chapter 8: *Transpersonal Responsibility*   120
- A. The Benefits of Civilization-Building   120
- B. Skeptical Views on Civilization-Building   123
- C. The Freudian Position   124
- D. Sex and Cultural Achievement   126
- E. Sexual Morality Today and Tomorrow   133

Index of Names   137
Index of Subjects   141
Table of Cases   147

Preface

This book is written by a lawyer, but is not addressed primarily to a legal audience. It takes an interdisciplinary approach to the problem of responsibility. The exposition strives to bring home to the lawyer the moral, social, and political dimensions of the subject, in addition to its legal aspects. At the same time it seeks to acquaint the non-lawyer with the legal side of responsibility in a manner which avoids professional technicalities as much as possible.

It is clear that this approach makes necessary excursions into various branches of learning. My statements on modern physics have been corroborated by my son, Peter H. Bodenheimer, who is Professor of Astrophysics at the University of California at Santa Cruz. My wife, Brigitte M. Bodenheimer, who taught Family Law for many years, has made valuable suggestions concerning questions of responsibility in personal and family relations. My contacts with existential psychiatry and one of its founders, Viktor E. Frankl, have aided my explorations of certain relations between law and forensic psychiatry.

In this day and age, the nondiscriminatory use of gender words presents an ubiquitous predicament for the writer. This book deals with persons rather than things; I realize that in many places such phrases as "he or she" or "his or her" would have been appropriate in meeting the problem. Because of the awkwardness of this technique, I have followed the view, with some departures, that the masculine is the unmarked gender in the English language. I am certain that this position will have no inhibiting effect upon the equal treatment of the sexes, in which I firmly believe.

Davis, California　　　　　　　　　　　　Edgar Bodenheimer
August 1979

PHILOSOPHY OF RESPONSIBILITY

Introductory Statement

The problem of responsibility is of encompassing significance today. Are we preparing ourselves for a productive and meaningful life? Are we educating our children to become respected and self-respecting members of the community? Are we treating our fellow human beings the way we ourselves would wish to be treated? Are we protecting our environment and natural resources from avoidable deterioration? Are we exercising our political rights in a manner that will secure a future for the human race? The answer to all of these crucial questions depends on how we conceive our responsibilities toward ourselves, toward other human beings, and toward the basic values of our existence.

The consciousness of responsibility faces a crisis today in the United States and in other countries. Serious crime and delinquency have soared in recent decades; corruption is widespread in politics, business, and labor organizations; violence mars the educational process in our schools; work morale has suffered a marked decline; the struggle of interest groups often exceeds the bounds of healthy social conflict. A widely held philosophy of undiluted self-seeking has played a part in bringing about this state of affairs. Unless we match the rights and liberties we claim for ourselves by self-imposed obligations designed to assume personal and social responsibilities, the disintegration of our society becomes a distinct possibility.

The widely-accepted doctrine of universal determinism has

put in question the very possibility of responsible conduct. Human decisions are always directed towards the future; they presuppose the making of choices between alternative courses of action. A mechanistic view of the world influenced by Newtonian cosmology has declared such choices to be illusory. Under this view, every action seemingly directed to the future is held to be ineluctably controlled by a rigid causal nexus reaching back into the past. It is obvious that individual responsibility becomes a fiction under such an assumption.

An attempt will be made in this work to restore a meaningful concept of responsibility. It will be shown that recent developments in the natural sciences have cast grave doubt on the truth of determinism conceived as a universally valid doctrine. Post-Einsteinian physics has propounded a notion of causality which preserves the possibility of free and responsible action. Such new findings have not as yet been sufficiently utilized in the social sciences, including criminology.

Part I of the book deals with the meaning, roots, and limits of the concept of responsibility. It contains a reevaluation of the freewill problem and its bearing on legal and moral responsibility. It also discusses the extent to which mental disorders should terminate or diminish criminal liability.

Part II of the book analyzes the various types of responsibility, ranging from accountability to oneself and members of one's family to social and transpersonal responsibility. An attempt is made to present a broad spectrum of the problem which brings together legal, moral, social, and political considerations.

PART I

A General Theory of Responsibility

CHAPTER 1

The Meaning and Roots of Responsibility

A. THE MEANING OF RESPONSIBILITY

Although the etymological derivation of a concept is not an infallible guide to the determination of its meaning, it often furnishes a useful clue in the endeavor to attain this objective. The term "responsibility" is derived from the verb "to respond," which in turn has its linguistic roots in the Latin word *respondere*. This word assumed a special significance in Roman law. A defendant, or his representative in court, "responded" to a complaint filed against him by putting forth reasons and arguments designed to meet the plaintiff's charges and to justify his own conduct. If these reasons and arguments were found unsatisfactory by the court, the defendant was required to answer to the complaint in a different and nonverbal way: he was called upon, perhaps, to "respond" in damages for a breach of contract, or to return some goods unlawfully appropriated by him. In a criminal case, when the defendant was unable to offer a satisfactory excuse for the unlawful act for which he was called to account, he was made to "answer" for his dereliction by the payment of a fine, by imprisonment, or by capital punishment.

The Romans also had an institution with authority to hold an individual responsible for breach of an obligation within the framework of social morality rather than law. During the period of the Roman Republic, two officials called censors were elected by the people for limited periods of time. In addition to being charged with taking the census, these officers exercised supervision over the morals of governmental functionaries and private citizens. In the census lists made up by them, they could affix a mark of censure (called *nota*) to a man's name if they disapproved of his conduct. This might happen, for example, if a man seriously mistreated his wife or divorced her without consulting a family council; if he neglected the education of his children or failed to honor his parents; if he followed a disreputable trade; if he was a spendthrift or led a profligate life; if an offical of the government was slovenly in the performance of his duties or accepted improper gifts; and if an official misused his public powers. Affixation of a *nota* operated as a form of public reprimand, but the censors also had the power of demoting the person in question to membership in a less respected *tribus* (a political subdivision of the Roman city state), an action which would, among other things, adversely affect his voting rights.[1]

There were no restrictions as to the reasons for which the censors might express their disapproval. This was one of the factors which induced the Romans to associate the censorial power with the field of morality rather than law. Moral codes are normally kept more vague than legal codes, so that the grounds for moral disapproval are frequently not clearly specified.[2] Furthermore, the sanctions which could be used by the censors were not regarded as legal sanctions, because they did not fall within the recognized categories of such sanctions. Their imposition or nonimposition was entirely within the discretion of the censors and, in contrast to legal sanctions, had no binding effect for the future. There also was no formal hearing and judicial-type judgment, although the person

---

1. On the institution of censorship in Rome see H. JOLOWICZ, HISTORICAL INTRODUCTION TO THE STUDY OF ROMAN LAW 50-51 (2d ed. 1965); 2 T. MOMMSEN, RÖMISCHES STAATSRECHT 363-393 (2d. ed. 1877).

2. The Chinese *Li*, for example, which is a set of ethical precepts, has been characterized as "rules, *partly defined and partly undefined*, of correct conduct and good manners, based more on moral principles than on conventions, and enforced not by legal sanction but by social reprobation." T. CHENG, CHINA MOULDED BY CONFUCIUS 37 (1947) (Emphasis supplied).

Ch. 1 The Meaning and Roots of Responsibility

charged with immoral conduct was given a chance to answer the accusation.

The main similarity between a legal trial and a proceeding before the censor lay in the fact that in both instances the obligation of a person to "respond" to a charge involved, first, a request by the authorities to justify conduct alleged to have been improper and, second, submission to some adverse consequences in case of failure to establish the propriety of such conduct. With the advent of Christianity in Western civilization, much emphasis was placed on the view that an individual is responsible for his actions not only to secular authorities and his fellowmen, but also to God, and that he faces Divine retribution for transgressions against moral precepts. The voice of God was deemed audible in the admonitions of the human conscience; responsibility was in an important sense conceived as an accounting for actions which was addressed by an individual to the tribunal of his conscience. In secularized versions of morality, such as the Kantian philosophy, it was autonomous human reason rather than heteronomous Divine reason that was seen mirrored in the promptings of conscience. This shift in thinking was not of a radical nature, since the autonomous moral sense of human beings was deemed by Kant and his followers to be essentially in harmony with the commands of a Supreme Being as understood by the Judaeo-Christian religious tradition.

To the legal and moral conceptions of responsibility must be added an existential and a social component of its meaning.[3] The existentialist philosophers, such as Sartre, Jaspers, and Heidegger, have stressed the responsibility which an individual bears for the shaping of his own existence.[4] Human beings should develop their latent capacities by sustained effort

---

3. This fourfold classification has not been strictly followed in Part II, entitled "The Varieties of Responsibility." Chapters 5 and 6, dealing with human relationships of various degrees of intimacy, take up both the moral and legal ramifications of such relationships. Chapter 4 discusses existential responsibility. Chapters 7 and 8 are concerned with social responsibility, in its personal and transpersonal aspects.

4. For general introductions to existentialism see M. WARNOCK, EXISTENTIALISM (1970); H. BARNES, AN EXISTENTIALIST ETHICS (1967); J. WILD, THE CHALLENGE OF EXISTENTIALISM (1955).

and become "authentic" persons. While this responsibility involves primarily the relation of an individual to himself, its successful exercise will also benefit others.

Under ordinary circumstances, an individual can attain his self-fulfillment only by productive work within a social framework. It is anticipated by society that the individual will use his capabilities and talents in the service of an organized community, whatever its nature and size may be, and make some contribution to the enterprise of civilization-building. Whenever a person has decided to perform a certain social task, he assumes a responsibility for the proper discharge of his functions or commitments. Such social responsibility takes on a political coloration if the mandate which society has entrusted to the individual involves the discharge of governmental leadership functions; in that event the relevant type of responsibility is that of a wielder of power towards the persons and groups that are subject to his authority or directly affected by its exercise.

The question must be asked whether these different categories of responsibility exhibit any unifying traits which warrant the use of a general and single term embracing all of these varieties. In other words, is there any common denominator leading some degree of homogeneity to the legal, moral, existential, and social manifestations of the idea of responsibility?

It may be said that such a bond of uniformity exists in the requirement that the responsible individual, in whatever sphere the problem of responsibility becomes relevant, must "answer" or "account" for something he has done or omitted to do. This answering and accounting will usually take the form of a justification. The person in question will attempt to demonstrate to himself or others that he weighed the consequences of his conduct and acted from ethically defensible motives; or else, he may wish to show that his action or failure to act was unavoidable under the circumstances.

The concept of responsibility also implies that the detrimental consequences of a person's actions are normally imputed to him. This imputation in many instances leads to the imposition of sanctions, whether these be of a legal or merely social nature. The person held responsible in a legal sense may be subjected to some form of punishment or an obligation to repair the damage done. A community judgment that an individual has infringed his moral obligations may result in some withdrawal of respect or, in serious cases, to at least temporary social ostracism. Failure to respond adequately to the vocational call which society has made on one of its members may entail the sanction of removal from an occupational (including a political) position. The relevant sanction for disregard of existential responsibilities tends to be personal unhappiness for neglecting to develop one's potentialities.

B. RESPONSIBILITY AND BLAMEWORTHINESS

The imputation of responsibility to a person in common understanding presupposes that this person had a volitional choice to avoid the action for which he is held to account. It is futile to fasten responsibility upon an automaton or robot who could not help doing what he did. When a person is called upon to answer for a dereliction, it is generally assumed that he was at fault in committing it. In other words, we are inclined to link the concept of responsibility to the notion of blameworthiness.

This observation applies in varying degrees to all forms of responsibility. A person is held morally responsible for an action detrimental to others if it is believed that he could have chosen a more acceptable alternative. In the area of law, responsibility is as a general rule tied to culpability, although the rubrics of culpability in many instances cover not only intentional but also negligent conduct.[5] Attribution of responsibility to a person for inadequate performance of a social task becomes meaningless if performance was impossible due to circumstances beyond the person's control. Existential responsibility for self-perfection is an empty demand if an individual, because of inherited and fixed character traits, is incapable of improvement.

In law, the term "responsibility" is sometimes applied to liability without fault; such an application of the term carries

---

5. For a position opposed to criminalization of negligent conduct see Hall, *Negligent Behavior Should be Excluded from Penal Liability*, 63 COLUM. L. REV. 632 (1963).

no moral but only a causal connotation.[6] Responsibility is also used in a purely causal sense in situations outside the range of the law. Thus, a statement may be found in a newspaper that the speech of a high government official explaining the state of the economy was "responsible" for a sharp drop in stock prices. We sometimes use the word "responsible" even with reference to the causation of events by nonhuman agencies. We may say, for example, that a heavy storm was responsible for the loss of a ship, or that the bad condition of a road was responsible for an automobile accident.[7] This morally neutral concept of responsibility will not be dealt with in this volume.

C. THE ROOTS OF RESPONSIBILITY

The question must be raised whether responsibility is in the main an artificial device invented by the powerful few to keep a measure of behavioral control over the many, or whether it is a postulate which is anchored in the structure of the human personality itself. It is noteworthy that at least one philosopher advocated a rejection of the concept of responsibility in all of its ethical and social ramifications. Max Stirner took the position that an individual had a right to do whatever he pleased in order to satisfy his natural desires, and that he owed no obligations of any kind either to himself or to his fellow human beings. To him, man has no special calling beyond "consuming" all the possibilities and temptations of life through unrestrained self-enjoyment, appropriating all that was within his power to obtain, and honoring no laws except those he had given to himself.[8] Stirner was convinced that society had arbitrarily placed barriers in the path of man's natural inclinations.

The position of Stirner that an individual has no responsibilities towards himself ignores the fact that everybody starts out in life as an imperfect being who will accomplish

---

6. For a position rejecting imposition of strict liability in criminal law see E. BODENHEIMER, TREATISE ON JUSTICE 202-210 (1967); J. HALL, GENERAL PRINCIPLES OF CRIMINAL LAW 342-351 (2d ed. 1960).

7. See H.L.A. HART, PUNISHMENT AND RESPONSIBILITY 214-215 (1968).

8. M. STIRNER, THE EGO AND HIS OWN 289, 296-297, 316-320, 186-190 (S. Byington transl. 1963).

Ch. 1 The Meaning and Roots of Responsibility

anything that is useful and worthwhile, even from pure self-interest, only by hard work, physical and mental growth, and self-discipline. This type of existential responsibility is a response to our inner striving to transcend the limits of our physiological appetites and develop our personality in all of its potentialities. Eminent psychiatrists have told us that everyone has in himself a drive for self-perfection, an urge for achievement which gives meaning to our life, although this impulse may need some stimulation from outside to keep it from being smothered by our instincts on the lower level.[9]

Stirner, in portraying man as a pure self-seeker and egoist, also ignored the fact that there is a social component in the human makeup which is reflected in the workings of human reason. The voice of reason—which in Freudian terminology is called the "reality principle"[10]—tells us that we have to adjust our conduct to the interests and wellbeing of others, lest we suffer harm from disregarding their justified claims. In the absence of mutual concern, our own desire for safety and convenience could simply not be realized. This consideration has given birth to a moral principle of almost universal recognition, which is called the Golden Rule. This rule, in its negative formulation, enjoins us "not to do to others what you do not want done to yourself." In its positive version, the rule exhorts us "to do to others as you would have them do to you." In most instances, the practical consequences of using the negative or positive version do not differ substantially, since much depends upon how the moral issue calling for application of the rule is semantically defined.[11]

The Golden Rule was proclaimed, in either its positive or negative form, in the Apocrypha, the New Testament, the

---

9. See *infra* Chapter 4 (D and E).
10. S. FREUD, BEYOND THE PLEASURE PRINCIPLE 5 (C. Hubback transl. 1922); FREUD, NEW INTRODUCTORY LECTURES ON PSYCHO-ANALYSIS 106 (W. Sprott transl. 1933).
11. If I say to myself "I do not wish others to refuse me aid when I need it; therefore I will not refuse aid to others when they need it," I am relying on the negative version of the Golden Rule. If I say to myself "I want others to come to my aid when I need it; therefore I shall come to the aid of others when they need it," I am relying on the positive version of the rule.

Analects of Confucius, the Indian Mahabharata, and the Buddhist Dhammapada.[12] Thomas Hobbes pronounced the rule to be "a law of nature,"[13] John Stuart Mill adopted it as the supreme ideal of utilitarian morality,[14] and Immanuel Kant, in a more abstract and less suggestive formulation, gave it expression in his categorical imperative.[15] John Locke once remarked that, as long as the Golden Rule was available, it was not of primary importance to write a speculative treatise on ethics.[16] The American sociologist Robert MacIver has argued that the Golden Rule is "the only ethical principle.... that can have a clear right of way everywhere in the kind of world we have inherited."[17]

To vindicate the truth of the Golden Rule, it is not necessary to have recourse to religious or metaphysical arguments. The rule has a strong empirical foundation in the typical reactions of individuals to the behavior of others who seek to destroy them, to cause pain or bodily harm to them, or to deceive their legitimate expectations. But in order to make the Golden Rule impregnable as a general principle of ethical conduct, its empirical base needs to be reinforced by a supporting act of our reasoning faculty. Our voice of reason tells us that our reactions to the offensive behavior of others are not unique, but are shared by all or most of our fellowmen. If I insist on respect for my own feelings and due recognition of my rights as an individual, it would seem to be an elementary command of common sense and fairness to accord an equal respect to the personality of other human beings.

We encounter here an element of moral perception which is inborn in man, although it may require fostering and

---

12. Tobit 4:15; Matth. 7:12; CONFUCIUS, ANALECTS XII:2 (A. Waley ed. 1938); Mahabharata 13, 113, 9; Dhammapada X. 129-139.

13. T. HOBBES, LEVIATHAN, Ch. 26 (Everyman's Lib. ed. 1914, p. 144).

14. J. MILL, UTILITARIANISM 22 (O. Piest ed. 1957).

15. I. KANT, FUNDAMENTAL PRINCIPLES OF THE METAPHYSICS OF MORALS 38 (T. Abbott transl. 1949): "Act only on that maxim whereby thou canst at the same time will that it should become a universal law."

16. See Smith, *Ethics*, in 5 ENCYCLOPEDIA OF THE SOCIAL SCIENCES 603 (1931).

17. MacIver, *The Deep Beauty of the Golden Rule*, in MORAL PRINCIPLES OF ACTION 43 (R. Anshen ed. 1952).

Ch. 1 The Meaning and Roots of Responsibility

stimulation to become fully developed. We have the capacity—some persons have it more than others—to abstract from our own selves, to put ourselves in the position of others, to perceive our own feelings and emotions, and to gain insight into those of other human beings. This capacity enables us—within limits—to view our relationships to others in an objective light. When we analyze these relationships in a detached fashion, we must necessarily come to the conclusion that certain moral principles of action and restraint are indispensable to make life bearable in human communities.

We must then reach the conclusion that the principle of responsibility has its roots in both the individual and social components of human nature. It acts as a spur to personal growth and self-actualization. It reminds us at the same time that we depend for our growth and self-actualization upon contact and interaction with other human beings, whose goodwill towards us is strongly influenced by the attitude we display towards them.

In addition to the duties which an individual owes to himself and others, the present work recognizes a further kind of responsibility which has received little attention in the pertinent literature. It is called "transpersonal responsibility" and may be defined as an individual's obligation to promote the values of human civilization in its technological and cultural aspects.[18] Enhancement of the amenities of life, furtherance of knowledge and control of nature, reflection on human individual and social life, and the creation of works of art and beauty have provided some of the greatest satisfactions of human beings. A specific responsibility to take part in the task of civilization-building should therefore be recognized. This responsibility is rooted in the highest and most distinctively human capacities of the spirit which throughout the course of history have striven to overcome the confining bounds of pure animal existence and mere physical survival.

---

18. See *infra* Chapter 8.

CHAPTER 2

Responsibility and Freewill

A. THE RELEVANCE OF FREEWILL

It was pointed out in the preceding chapter that in situations in which the problem of responsibility arises, a person must "answer" or "account" for something which that person has done or decided to do. In order to meet the tests of responsible behavior, the actor must ordinarily show that he weighed the consequences of his conduct, considered the effect it might have on other persons, and scrutinized possible alternatives. In discharging this burden, it will often be necessary for the person in question to convince others that he was motivated by certain principles of action which from an ethical point of view are, or should be, worthy of respect. If he is unable to meet this burden, he is likely to be blamed for not having lived up to the standards of responsibility. If the actor happens to be a determinist, however, he may shrug off a charge of irresponsible behavior with the remark: "I could not help doing what I did. Considering my genetic endowment and the conditions of my past and present environment, I have no doubt that my action was unavoidable."

It would seem that responsibility, in any morally meaningful sense, is destroyed if a radically deterministic position is taken. If human actions are automatic responses to preceding causal pressures, if under given conditions only one action is possible for a person, it is futile to level criticism or blame at such a person. A death blow is administered under that theory to the

Ch. 2 *Responsibility and Freewill*

entire notion of moral responsibility.[1] A severe cloud is also cast over the institution of punishment if impossibility of moral choice is assumed. Under the deterministic view, an offender against the law may suffer highly unpleasant and disadvantageous consequences, like long-term imprisonment, for an action into which an unfortunate temperament or an infelicitous life history had propelled him by an unbreakable chain of compulsive causality.

It has, however, been argued that no irreconcilable conflict exists between the deterministic philosophy and the institution of punishment. This argument takes as its starting point the consideration that punishment, or the threat of it, provides a motive for conduct. Hence, the possibility of punishment for unlawful acts may cause people to refrain from such acts. If this potential motivation turns out to be inoperative in a particular case, the imposition of punishment upon a person who has failed to respond to its threat remains fully justified according to this view. It is assumed that the behavior of the offender can be altered in the future by the infliction of punishment, which in that event operates itself as a determining factor. Furthermore, other persons in society may be deterred by the punishment of offenders from committing similar acts.[2]

This attempt to demonstrate compatibility between the belief in determinism and the institution of punishment is not convincing. It is obvious that, from the vantage point of a consistent deterministic philosophy, the individual offender was not, and could not have been, deterred from the commission of the crime for which he was punished. His action followed with cast-iron necessity from a web of causes preceding it. Strict determinists have therefore taken the position that a criminal offender cannot be held responsible for what he did. Robert Fearey has given expression to this point of view in a radical formulation:

> While no man in his right mind would think of blaming a ten-year-old car for bad performance, an

---

1. See Branden, *Free Will, Moral Responsibility and the Law*, 42 SO. CAL. L. REV. 264, 265 (1969).
2. See M. SCHLICK, PROBLEMS OF ETHICS 152 (1939); P. NOWELL-SMITH, ETHICS 303-304 (1954). This view is also implicit in John

adult criminal is everywhere considered responsible for his crimes, with only a partial bow toward the inherited, environmental, and other passively acquired characteristics which, together with a possible soul, in fact entirely account for his waywardness. Man's variegated character and wide capacities have blinded us to the fact that he is in fact as passive to his creation and development, and hence as unaccountable for his actions, as an inanimate machine.[3]

If we punish an offender notwithstanding the fact that he had no alternative to the commission of his crime, the only possible defense of such action was pointed out by Justice Holmes. A convicted criminal, he said, may be innocent in a moral sense of the term, but we may liken his position to that of a soldier dying for his country. Society may treat the criminal as a means to an end, it may sacrifice him to the exigencies of the public welfare. The public welfare is promoted by the fact that punishment may serve to discourage other members of society from committing crimes. Furthermore, the isolation of the criminal in prison increases the safety of society, at least for a time. In the view of Holmes, if the offense committed by the wrongdoer was unavoidable, society's response to the offense must also be regarded as unavoidable because it constitutes an act of collective self-defense.[4]

To argue, as Holmes does, that a helpless victim of circumstances may be sacrificed for the good of society is obviously a very hardheaded position. Nathaniel Branden denounced punishment based on such a theory as "sheer brutality."[5] The position of Holmes could perhaps be accepted if no reasonable alternative could be discerned. One theoretical alternative would be the abolition of the institution of

---

Stuart Mill's essay *An Examination of Sir William Hamilton's Philosophy*, in FREE WILL 62-65 (S. Morgenbesser & J. Walsh eds. 1962).

3. Fearey, *The Concept of Responsibility*, 45 J. CRIM. L., CRIMIN. & POL. SCI. 21, 24 (1954).

4. O. HOLMES, THE COMMON LAW 42-47 (1923); 1 HOLMES-LASKI LETTERS 806 (M. Howe ed. 1953).

5. Branden, *supra* note 1, at 265.

punishment. No country on this globe has thus far taken this step, and there are no indications, in the United States or elsewhere, that punishment will be eliminated in the foreseeable future.[6] The other alternative is to subject the doctrine of determinism, which is still widely accepted by psychiatrists and criminologists, especially in the Anglo-American orbit, to a fresh scrutiny in the light of recent developments in the natural and social sciences. This avenue will be pursued in the remaining parts of this chapter.

B. CAUSAL LAWS AND CAUSAL OCCURRENCES

Determinism has been described as the doctrine that the human will is subject to the law of causality.[7] This statement is ambiguous unless the term "law of causality" is explained further. The phrase may mean merely that every event, natural as well as human, has a cause in the sense that it would not have happened in the absence of a preceding event which produced or at least contributed to its occurrence. This conception of causality provides an insufficient foundation for determinism. Determinism presupposes more than a finding that event B would not have occurred in the absence of event A. It assumes further that, whenever an event, or a particular combination of events, takes place in reality, a certain effect will ensue with inexorable necessity according to the operation of invariable laws. If the principle of causality is formulated in this fashion, causality becomes coterminous with determinism.

Many philosophers and scientists of the past have adopted this last-mentioned view of causality. Kant, for example, was convinced that, in the empirical world of nature, everything that happens is determined by necessary laws which allow of no exceptions. He said:

> Every cause presupposes a rule according to which certain appearances follow as effects; and

---

6. The same conclusion was reached by J. ANDENAES, PUNISHMENT AND DETERRENCE 155-159 (1974).

7. Rée, *Determinism and the Illusion of Moral Responsibility*, in A MODERN INTRODUCTION TO PHILOSOPHY 10 (3rd ed. by P. Edwards and A. Pap 1973).

every rule requires uniformity in the effects. This uniformity is, indeed, that upon which the concept of a cause ... is based.[8]

Schopenhauer asserted that all causes are compelling causes and that, whenever they emerge, they will produce a certain effect with undeviating regularity.[9] "Everything that happens, from the largest to the smallest, happens necessarily."[10] This widely-held belief was strongly influenced by Sir Isaac Newton's conception of the cosmos. According to Newton, nature is governed by mechanical laws which operate without fail. Uniform causes produce uniform effects, and there are no exceptions from the validity and operation of the causal principle understood in this sense. Kant argued that Newtonian mechanistic causality did not necessarily apply to human beings; in his opinion, human beings were not only creatures of physical nature but also belonged to a second world, the world of reason and the spirit, which was exempt from the rigid principles of deterministic causality.[11] Other philosophers, however, and many scientists, sociologists, and psychiatrists were convinced that human beings, like inanimate things, plants, and animals, were part of the empirical world of nature and fully controlled by the laws governing nature.[12]

Developments in the natural sciences during the twentieth century have subjected the workings and scope of the causal principle to searching scrutiny. In the domain of physics, the

---

8. I. KANT, CRITIQUE OF PURE REASON 473-474 (N. Smith transl. 1950). See also *id.* at 466: "That all events in the sensible world stand in thoroughgoing connection in accordance with unchangeable laws of nature is an established principle of the Transcendental Analytic and allows of no exceptions."

9. A. SCHOPENHAUER, ESSAY ON THE FREEDOM OF THE WILL 7-8 (K. Kolenda transl. 1960).

10. *Id.* at 62.

11. KANT, *supra* note 8, at 476-478.

12. See, for example, Freud, *The Unconscious,* in THE MAJOR WORKS OF SIGMUND FREUD 454 (Great Books of the Western World v. 54, 1952): "Anyone ... breaking away from the determination of natural phenomena, at any single point, has thrown over the whole scientific outlook on the world." See also *id.* at 486, where Freud expresses his belief that determinism governs even mental life.

Ch. 2 Responsibility and Freewill

observation of seemingly random movements in subatomic nature has led some physicists and philosophers of science to the conclusion that the causal principle should be abandoned altogether. It is their view that occurrences in microphysics are governed by chance; they believe that such regularity and predictability as exists in large-scale, macrophysical phenomena should be attributed to the operation of the statistical laws of averages, which are not causal laws in the strict sense of the term.[13] Einstein combatted this view, being convinced that "God does not throw dice."[14] He maintained his conviction in the general validity of the causal principle, assuming that seeming departures from it were attributable to the inexactness of our observations and measuring instruments.[15]

More recently, a number of other scientists have returned to a belief in the reality of causality in microcosmic nature, as viewed through the prism of the quantum theory, without having thus far been able to corroborate their findings by irrefutable evidence.[16] These scientists do not assume, however, that causality reigns supreme in physical nature. The existence of a certain amount of chance in natural events is being presupposed, although chance is identified less with arbitrary randomness than with the crossing and possible interpenetration of numerous causal chains. Because of the unique and highly complex way in which different lines of development become entangled in such confluences, the discovery of any direct, linear-type cause-effect relationship becomes illusory; it has also been found impossible to detect any cast-iron laws controlling complex causal interconnections.[17]

---

13. N. Bohr, Atomic Theory and the Description of Nature 4 (1934); R. Von Mises, Probability, Statistics and Truth 209-210, 220, 223 (2d ed. by H. Geiringer 1957); B. Russell, Philosophy 294 (1927).

14. Reported by W. Heisenberg, Physics and Beyond 80 (1971).

15. Einstein, Prologue to M. Planck, Where Is Science Going 11 (1932).

16. D. Bohm, Causality and Chance in Modern Physics Chs. I, IV and V (1957); M. Born, Natural Philosophy of Cause and Chance 3-4 (1949); M. Bunge, Causality 14-15 (1959).

17. See Bohm, *supra* note 16, at 3, 7, 9, 19-20; Bunge, *supra* n. 16, at 124.

Taking the example of the weather, for example, its state at any particular time is produced by a number of contingencies, such as atmospheric pressure, direction of the wind, moisture of the air, temperature, size and density of the clouds, and other factors. The coincidence and interaction of these factors at each moment is not governed by any discernible laws; this makes weather prediction (at least under complex atmospheric conditions) a hazardous undertaking. As Bunge points out, "as soon as the possibility of a plurality of causes (or effects) is admitted, the picture of the causal chain ceases to be a possible model of becoming."[18] When various thrusts of activity and reactivity cross and interpenetrate each other, the notion of a simple, inevitable cause-effect relationship ceases to be practically useful.

Post-Einsteinian developments in physics have suggested a strong possibility that the abandonment of strict determinism does not necessarily lead to the conclusion that God is playing dice in dealing with the world. The distinguished German physicist Max Born has made a fundamental distinction between two types of causality.[19] Among the examples he recited to illustrate the first type of causality are the following: (1) Chemical reactions are caused by the affinity of molecules, and (2) Wars are caused by economic conditions (a proposition believed in by economic determinists). These two statements are meant to articulate general, infallible laws which the maker of the statement holds to be true in all instances. Other examples of such laws are the observations that water cooled below a certain temperature becomes a solid, and that an egg left in boiling water for a certain time will get hard. Here it is particularly clear that, given the existence of certain conditions, certain effects will follow with absolute necessity, due to a law of nature.

The second type of causality, according to Born, is exemplified by statements such as "The Indian famine of 1946 was caused by a bad harvest" and "The American war of secession was caused by the economic situation in the slave states." These sentences are not meant to give expression to universally valid laws; they are designed to trace the

---

18. BUNGE, *supra* note 16, at 124.
19. BORN, *supra* note 16, at 5-9.

individualized causes of single events. The maker of the first statement does not suggest that bad harvests will invariably produce famines; the stricken nation may be able to prevent starvation by imports of grain. The maker of the second statement may not believe in a sociological law to the effect that all wars are caused by economic conditions; he is merely enunciating his view as to the particular cause responsible for the outbreak of the American war of secession.

There is not as yet available a generally accepted terminology for distinguishing between the two types of causality. Born speaks of causality expressing "timeless relations" and causality "referring to single events."[20] F.S.C. Northrop differentiates between "strong" and "weak" forms of causality.[21] One may also use the terms "deterministic causality" and "nondeterministic causality" to signify the distinction.

Whether or not the nondeterministic type of causality exists in nature is not entirely free from controversy. There are, however, a number of writers who believe that the principle of causality can be restored in quantum physics if the view is abandoned that everything that happens in nature is attributable to the operation of inflexible laws.[22] In Mario Bunge's formulation, "the usual interpretation of quantum mechanics does not sweep out causes and effects, but rather the rigid causal nexus among them."[23]

Regardless of whether or not nondeterministic causality occurs in nature, this type of causality will frequently be found in the making of human decisions. Suppose, for example, that an academic instructor receives offers for an appointment from two first-rate universities. Many good reasons may exist for the acceptance of either of these offers, and the relative strength of

---

20. *Id.* at 5, 9.
21. Northrop, *Causation, Determinism, and the 'Good'*, in DETERMINISM AND FREEDOM IN THE AGE OF SCIENCE 201, 208 (S. Hook ed. 1961).
22. See BOHM, *supra* note 16, at 141; Northrop, *supra* note 21, at 208-210; BUNGE, *supra* note 16, at 14-15.
23. BUNGE, *supra* note 16, at 14-15. Bunge quotes a statement by St. Thomas Aquinas (SUMMA THEOLOGICA, Pt. I, Qu. CXV, Art. 6): "It is not true that, given any cause whatever, the effect must follow of necessity." *Id.* at 103, n. 14.

these reasons may be assessed differently by the instructor at different times. The final decision made by him may be due to the incidence of highly individualized considerations. In that event it would not be possible to trace this decision to the operation of a universal causal law and to argue that the decision was "determined" in the sense that the decisionmaker had no choice in making it. In the area of judicial decisionmaking, when many conflicting interests have to be accommodated by a court, and where a number of general rules may be applicable to the situation, the resulting determination by the court is not uncaused; it is based on an evaluation of the weight of concrete facts rather than being dictated by an abstract, general rule of law. Numerous causal threads contribute to the making of a decision which bears no earmarks of imperative necessity.

The same considerations apply to situations in which a single cause, rather than a multiplicity of causes, explains the making of a decision. I may decide to travel to India because I am interested in studying Indian art. This would appear to be a free decision, because there is no ascertainable natural or social law which pushes me with irresistible force into making the journey. The wide range of such decisions in human life has not been sufficiently emphasized in the social and behavioral sciences because the novel distinction made in the natural sciences between causality produced by rigid laws and the looser forms of causality has not as yet filtered down into these areas of human thought.

We may thus assume that, before a human action is taken, the decisionmaker had before him, in many instances, several possibilities of acting. After the action was taken, on the other hand, it became a necessary action; it formed part of a chain of causation which can no longer be undone. Differently expressed, from hindsight everything is determined.[24]

C. CAUSES AND REASONS

We generally speak of cause in reference to some event or occurrence, or some human act or omission, which brings

---

24. The reason why so many psychiatrists are determinists may, at least in part, be explained by the fact that they are dealing with the past

about a certain effect or consequence. Sometimes we use the term reason as a synonym for cause. Thus we might say that throwing a match into a haystack was the reason for a fire which destroyed a barn. But since the term reason is closely related to the activity of reasoning, there are good grounds for limiting it, at least in a scholarly vocabulary, to situations in which a human being justifies, to himself or others, a decision or action he has taken in the past or will take in the future. Differently expressed, a reason for action in this restricted sense is "something which is relevant to the promotion of some purpose known to be pursued by human beings."[25]

It has been pointed out that causes of events frequently produce their effect through the operation of general laws; when a metal is heated, it will expand. On the other hand, the reasons justifying a human action (which may also be called motives) are normally of an individualized nature. I may decide to comply with the legal rules proscribing violence because I consider them reasonable, or because I am afraid of going to prison, or because I do not want to lose my friends. I set myself a purpose which will govern my future conduct. There is nothing automatic in such a decision; a determinist would be hard put to prove that it must be attributed to the workings of an inexorable law.

D. THE BATTLE OF MOTIVES

The problem of freewill is by no means solved by the conclusion that the causes of human actions do not necessarily compel such actions by the operation of rigid physical or psychological laws. Other theories leading to a denial of human decisional freedom have been put forth which require attention and examination.

One of these theories is based on the conviction that, in the

---

history of the patient. After the choices which the patient may at one time have had eventuated in actual decisions or actions, the causal nexus became closed. See in this connection P. WEISS, NATURE AND MAN 10 (1947).

25. H. HART AND A. HONORÉ, CAUSATION IN THE LAW 53 (1959). The conclusions reached by these authors on the distinction between causes and reasons are similar to mine. For a different approach see Davidson, *Actions, Reasons, and Causes*, 60 J. PHILOS. 685 (1963).

battle of motivations preceding a human decision, the outcome of the battle is determined by the irresistible impact of the strongest motive, or strongest combination of motives. In the words of Robert Blatchford:

> In all cases the action of the will depends upon the relative strength of two or more motives. The stronger motive decides the will; just as the heavier weight decides the balance of a pair of scales.[26]

This theory looks at motives as things-in-themselves, as reified entities which have an independent power to force themselves upon the human consciousness. From the point of view of common-sense psychology, it certainly seems odd to assert that motives make choices for us, and that we have no control over our motives. A person may hold this view, but he would be hard put to verify it. What our common experience suggests is that an individual confronted with a choice compares the consequences of alternative courses of action and evaluates the positive and negative aspects of these consequences. The self then determines what motive, or group of motives, tips the balance in favor of a certain action. The assignment of priority to a particular incentive for action does not necessarily remain uniform throughout the process of deliberation. A motive that appears to the decisionmaker to have a preponderant force on Monday may be relegated by him to a secondary position on Tuesday. It seems obvious in such cases that it is not the strongest motive that determines the decision of the person, but that his or her decision determines what the strongest motive shall be. In the words of Erich Fromm: "Where contradictory inclinations effectively operate within the personality, there is freedom of choice."[27]

There are situations where, in the battle of motives, one particular ground for pursuing a certain course of action is so strong, so dominant, so overpowering that one might be tempted to deny the existence of genuine choice. For example, when a prospective student is offered admission at an

---

26. Blatchford, *The Delusion of Free Will*, in PHILOSOPHY AND CONTEMPORARY ISSUES 18 (2d. ed. by J. Burr and M. Goldinger 1976).
27. E. FROMM, THE HEART OF MAN 143 (1964). Cf. R. EDWARDS, FREEDOM, RESPONSIBILITY AND OBLIGATION 11-12 (1969).

outstanding college as well as a mediocre one, an extremely high degree of predictability attends the decision which the student will make. But the fact that a decision is predictable does not mean that it is unfree. In some cases, a certain choice may be so unreasonable that it can be practically ruled out. In the example just given, however, it is not impossible that the student may choose the mediocre college for highly personal reasons, although this may produce a drawback for his future professional career.

Some post-Freudian authors have contended that the motivational process is unfree because the decisive motive may be an unconscious factor of which the acting person has no knowledge, and over which he therefore cannot possibly have control. This view was put forward in some detail by John Hospers, who expressed his belief that the range of unconscious motivation was very wide.[28] His mentor Freud, however, was much more cautious in his conclusions regarding this type of motivation, admitting that firm proof of the theory was available in only a few instances.[29] There may be some cases in which unconscious motivation plays havoc with a seemingly conscious choice; but there are others in which unconscious elements merely strengthen the final conscious decision of the actor because they form part of his personality structure, conceived as an integrated unit. As the psychiatrist Seymour Halleck has pointed out, there is no reason to assume that the unconscious by its very nature is a dangerous and unpredictable agent, "a lurking shadow hidden somewhere in the soul of each individual, waiting only for the opportunity to commit some heinous act."[30] There is no good ground to deny the responsibility of an individual if a decision is made by him after comparing the likely consequences of alternative choices, even though the outcome may be influenced by inner subterranean forces of which he is unaware. The existence of responsibility

---

28. Hospers, *What Means this Freedom?* in DETERMINISM AND FREEDOM IN THE AGE OF SCIENCE 126-127 (S. Hook ed. 1961).

29. Freud, *The Psychopathology of Everyday Life,* in 6 COMPLETE PSYCHOLOGICAL WORKS 254-256 (J. Strachey ed. 1960). Cf. E. BODENHEIMER, TREATISE ON JUSTICE 184-186 (1967).

30. S. HALLECK, PSYCHIATRY AND THE DILEMMAS OF CRIME 210 (1967).

may be seriously questioned, on the other hand, if there is convincing evidence that strong subconscious pressures simply drowned out, or rendered illusory, any conscious choice by the actor.

E. THE INDELIBLE CHARACTER

Even if it is admitted that in the battle of motivations the conscious ego in most cases makes the final decision, it may be argued that the character of the decisionmaker is so firmly shaped by genetic endowment and early environment that his choices are not real and genuine. Schopenhauer put forth this argument with great vigor and conviction. The character of an individual is constant, he said; it remains the same throughout the whole of life. A person never changes; as he or she acted in one case, so that person will always act again under equal circumstances. The proverb "Whoever steals once, remains a thief all his life" expresses an uncontestable truth for Schopenhauer.[31]

The correctness of this view is subject to serious doubt. Although the character of a person, as formed by heredity and early environment, places definite limits on that person's range of potentialities and choices, this does not mean that a person's character *per se* constitutes a straitjacket that inhibits decisional freedom in a radical manner. Although there may be individuals whose character is rigidly and impregnably fixed, experience suggests that, for the most part, a person's character is to some substantial extent malleable and amenable to change. It is true that the constitution of some persons renders them capable of making the requisite exertion and that of other persons does not. But the fact that some persons are equipped with greater will power than others does not offer any guaranty that they will actually employ their will power; self-improvement requires some conscious effort that may be omitted, although the potentiality for making it was present.

Blatchford disagrees with these conclusions. He is convinced that a person will choose "as heredity and environment cause him to choose."[32] This statement assumes that an individual is

---

31. SCHOPENHAUER, *supra* note 9, at 51-52.
32. Blatchford, *supra* note 26, at 18.

wholly passive towards his inherited traits and surrounding conditions. The well-known geneticist Dobzhansky, on the other hand, came to the conclusion that an individual learns to be the kind of person which he eventually becomes, and that he has the possibility of developing into any one of a great many different kinds of persons.[33] To be sure, which one he does become depends to a significant degree on the society in which he lives and on his genetic endowment. Heredity and environment tend to predispose a person towards certain types of conduct; they do not, in Dobzhansky's opinion, coerce such type of conduct. Thus, a certain decisional freedom must be added to heredity and environment as a third motivational force. "The ability of man to choose freely between ideas and acts is one of the fundamental characteristics of human evolution."[34] The same conclusion was reached by the psychiatrist Viktor Frankl, who declared that the human being is a product of heredity, environment, and self-determination.[35]

There certainly exists no generally valid proof to support Schopenhauer's belief that a person who once committed an act of larceny will remain a thief all his life. There are recidivists and nonrecidivists among criminals, and it has also been found that in many cases the criminal inclinations of an offender will erode and disappear with advancing age.

F. THE MODERN SYNTHESIS

The retreat from determinism which has been made possible by recent developments in natural science and psychology does not take us back to the classical view, espoused with particular forcefulness by Kant, that human beings, with the exception of extreme psychotics, are free and rational beings.[36] There are occurrences, especially in the purely

---

33. T. DOBZHANSKY, THE BIOLOGICAL BASIS OF HUMAN FREEDOM 53 (1956).
34. *Id.* at 134.
35. Frankl, *Grundriss der Existenzanalyse und Logotherapie*, in 3 HANDBUCH DER NEUROSENLEHRE UND PSYCHOTHERAPIE 683 (1959). See also V. FRANKL, THE WILL TO MEANING 16 (1970).
36. KANT, *supra* note 8, at 478: "Reason is present in all the actions of men at all times and under all circumstances, and is always the same." See also *id.* at 476.

physical sphere of human existence, which appear to be wholly determined, such as the invasion of the body by powerful germs and the illnesses resulting therefrom.[37] Kant would not have denied this fact. He was convinced, on the other hand, that in the psychological realm a lack of capacity to control the emotions by the restraining force of reason would exist only in relatively few abnormal persons. Modern psychology does not support him in this belief. For example, if an individual falls in love with a person of the opposite sex, a decision of reason to extinguish the feeling because it is unreciprocated is unlikely to have any appreciable effect. Emotions like anger, hatred, and jealousy may elude control if they reach a very high degree of intensity.

Human volitional freedom appears to be largest in the noetic sphere, which comprises the activities of the mind as distinguished from those of the body or psyche. The selection of a preferred philosophy or life style, although it may be influenced by personality makeup and social milieu, will often have the character of a predominantly free decision. The choice of an occupation is free within certain limits set by the individual's capabilities and, in many societies, his social origin. In the area of illegal behavior, the thoroughly premeditated assassination of a cruel despot, believed by the actor to be necessary in the interest of liberation and happiness of his people, may be the result of free and rational deliberation.

Many antisocial acts are probably produced by a blend of volitional freedom and causal pressure.[38] Early experiences and an infelicitous life history may have pushed an individual in the direction of delinquency; but the existence of the criminal law will normally exert a strong counterpressure against activation of sociopathic inclinations. In the ensuing battle of motives, the ultimate decision need not be conceived as automatic.[39]

---

37. Even in this area it is not clear whether and to what extent a firm determination to remain healthy may have some protective effect.

38. For a statement by a distinguished physicist affirming the complementarity of freedom and necessity see M. BORN, PHYSICS IN MY GENERATION 171-172 (2d. ed. 1969).

39. See *supra* under (D).

There are, however, cases in which the rational control function of a criminal offender has become immobilized or strongly reduced. The bearing of these cases upon the problem of responsibility will be discussed in the next chapter.

CHAPTER 3

The Limits of Responsibility

A. INTRODUCTORY OBSERVATIONS

It was pointed out in the preceding chapter that the present state of the physical and biological sciences permits us to recognize a meaningful concept of personal responsibility. This concept is based on a reasonable assumption that human beings normally possess the capacity to make choices between alternative courses of action and to arrive at decisions which are not forced upon them by extraneous factors. The significance of this assumption for the field of the law lies in the fact that it lends justification to the promulgation and imposition of punitive sanctions for engaging in socially proscribed conduct. It is anticipated that the threat of a sanction will induce a resolution on the part of most people to observe the norms of the law rather than to defy them. If the possibility of genuine human choices were denied, if it were believed that unlawful conduct is brought about by inexorable forces beyond the control of the lawbreaker, there would still be room for a system of quarantining socially dangerous persons; but the fundamental premises of a system of criminal law based on the institution of punishment would be thoroughly undermined.

Although in the early part of the twentieth century a few attempts were made to abolish the institution of punishment and to rest the administration of criminal law on the morally

Ch. 3 *The Limits of Responsibility* 31

neutral concept of "social dangerousness,"[1] such experiments turned out to be shortlived. It appears that, due to a deepseated and probably ineradicable prime instinct of mankind, the notion of punishment, linked with the ideas of blameworthiness and personal responsibility, forms an integral part of the criminal justice system throughout the world.[2]

The recognition of responsibility does not mean that human beings are held responsible by the law for every objectively unlawful act which they commit. Certain limits on responsibility have been established by all legal systems, although there exists considerable variation regarding the definition and scope of these limits.

B. VOLUNTARY AND INVOLUNTARY ACTS

Any system of law resting on the notion of responsibility will draw a distinction between voluntary and involuntary acts of wrongdoing; it will reserve the imputation of responsibility, with some exceptions, for the former. We find this distinction already in Plato's dialogue *The Laws*,[3] but his treatment of the legal consequences flowing from the distinction is complex and somewhat cryptic.[4] Aristotle's handling of the problem, on the other hand, is lucid and still helpful in gaining a proper perspective. In analyzing the conditions of responsibility, Aristotle pointed out that an action is voluntary if it is not done under compulsion or owing to ignorance.[5] By a compulsory

1. Examples are the Soviet Criminal Code of 1926 and the Cuban Code of Social Defense of 1936. Neither of them is in effect today.
2. A very useful research tool for the study of the criminal law of many countries is the volume entitled REFORM OF THE FEDERAL CRIMINAL LAWS: HEARING BEFORE THE SUBCOMMITTEE ON CRIMINAL LAWS AND PROCEDURES OF THE COMMITTEE ON THE JUDICIARY, UNITED STATES SENATE, 92d Congress, 2d Session (March 21, 1972), Part III, Subpart C (Comparative Law).
3. PLATO, THE LAWS, Bk. IX. 861-871 (R. Bury ed. 1942).
4. A detailed explanation of Plato's position is offered by Agretelis, *'Mens Rea' in Plato and Aristotle*, 1 ISSUES IN CRIMINOLOGY 19, 23-28 (1965).
5. ARISTOTLE, NICOMACHEAN ETHICS, Bk. III. i. 2-27 (Loeb Class. Lib. ed. 1947).

action he meant one solely due to external causes, "the person compelled contributing nothing to it."[6]

This raises the question whether a person acting under duress may be held responsible for his action. Suppose A forces B, under threat of immediate death in case of refusal, to kill C. Is B acting voluntarily in this situation? Aristotle exhibits some ambivalence in dealing with this question, arguing that there is a mixture of voluntary and involuntary elements present under these circumstances. His final conclusion is that the voluntary element is the prevailing one, since psychological compulsion (as distinguished from physical compulsion) does not destroy choice on the part of the person acting under duress.[7]

The second Aristotelian exemption from responsibility is ignorance. Ignorance meant to him an unawareness on the part of the actor of facts whose presence was an essential ingredient of the unlawful action.[8] An example would be the case of a hunter shooting a man in the woods, thinking he was a deer. Here the hunter was unaware of a fact essential to a finding of homicide, namely, the fact that the victim of the killing must be a human being.

Thus, as a matter of general theory, Aristotle holds a man morally, and presumably legally, responsible "if, and only if, with knowledge of the particular circumstances and in the absence of an external compulsion, he deliberately chooses (forms the intent) to do a particular act."[9]

The Aristotelian theory of responsibility anticipates some of the most essential requirements of the *mens rea* doctrine, which seems to have become part and parcel of all criminal justice systems.[10] As a general rule, a violation of the criminal law is punishable only if it was committed intentionally or recklessly, the latter term implying a conditional intent to accept the unlawful consequences of one's action should they occur. Some

---

6. *Id.* at i. 12. An example would be the situation in which A pushes B against C, so that C falls to the ground and is injured. Clearly B does not act voluntarily in this situation.

7. *Id.* at i. 2-6.

8. *Id.* at i. 13-15.

9. Agretelis, *supra* note 4, at 32.

10. This is a conclusion which can be drawn from a thorough study of the source materials in the volume cited *supra* note 2.

Ch. 3 The Limits of Responsibility

derelictions, however, are punishable if committed negligently, i.e., carelessly but without intent.[11]

Aristotle's ambivalent attitude concerning the defense of duress is mirrored in the position of different legal systems towards the problem. The common law does not excuse homicide committed on command and under threat of death. Other legal systems excuse the person acting under this kind of duress, subject perhaps to a few exceptions.[12] Ignorance or mistake regarding the existence of factual prerequisites of criminal liability appear to be regarded everywhere as a valid defense against conviction, at least when such ignorance or mistake nullifies the awareness of wrongdoing. But an assertion of ignorance of a criminal law will not be regarded as an excusing factor, except perhaps under narrowly circumscribed conditions.[13] Self-defense against unprovoked attack is everywhere regarded as a justification. Substantial disagreements exist, on the other hand, with respect to the prerequisites and scope of the defense of necessity, which relates to the commission of an unlawful act to save life, limb, or property of the actor or a member of his family from an acute danger.[14] Some of the defenses mentioned, such as self-defense and certain forms of necessity, duress, and mistake operate to negate some constitutive elements of a criminal offense, that is, the existence of a crime, rather than provide an excuse from otherwise illegal conduct.[15]

---

11. Jerome Hall has questioned the desirability of subjecting negligent conduct to criminal sanctions. See *supra* Ch. 1, n. 5.

12. See, for example, the German Criminal Code of 1871, as revised in 1975. While duress is generally recognized as a defense under that Code, there is an exception when the actor was obligated to cope with the danger because of some special relationship, or some other cogent reason. STRAFGESETZBUCH §35.

13. §17 of the German Criminal Code, *supra* note 12, excuses unavoidable instances of ignorance of the law. An example is lack of acquaintance with a specific regulatory law (such as a registration requirement) which had been insufficiently publicized. The position of courts in the United States is discussed by W. LAFAVE & A. SCOTT, HANDBOOK OF CRIMINAL LAW 356-369 (1972).

14. See the general discussion of the problem by E. BODENHEIMER, TREATISE ON JUSTICE 218-225 (1967).

15. The distinction between justifying and excusing conditions in

The detailed legal norms regarding these various limitations of criminal responsibility are a matter of positive law. They will not be analyzed in this general work on the philosophical foundations of responsibility. One exception from legal accountability, however, will be discussed in some detail, because it reaches into the core area of a philosophical anthropology concerned with the roots of human accountability. This is the problem of mental disease in its impact on legal responsibility. It is a problem which at least in the English-speaking world has engendered a great deal of heated controversy in recent decades.

C. THE REALITY OF MENTAL DISEASE

Until the 1960s, it was generally assumed that the existence of mental disease was an unquestionable phenomenon of human pathology. It was also firmly believed that persons suffering from the more severe forms of insanity should not be held liable under the criminal law, because the unlawful acts committed by such persons were the result of a serious pathological condition over which they had no control.

In 1961, the American psychiatrist Thomas Szasz published a book in which he bluntly declared that "mental disease is a myth."[16] Psychiatrists, he said, are in reality not dealing with mental illnesses; they are faced with their patients' personal, social, and ethical problems of living. Szasz also suggested that the belief in mental illness is socially deleterious, because it undermines the principle of responsibility upon which a democratic political system must necessarily be based.[17]

In a later work, Szasz conceded that there exist physical diseases of the brain which manifest themselves in mental symptoms. He adverted to, but rejected the view expressed by some psychiatrists that all mental diseases have a physiological basis. In his opinion, the large majority of so-called "mental illnesses," including the most common forms of paranoia and schizophrenia, merely represent unconventional modes of

---

criminal law is discussed by Fletcher, *The Individualization of Excusing Conditions*, 47 SO. CAL. L. REV. 1269 (1974).
16. T. SZASZ, THE MYTH OF MENTAL ILLNESS 296 (1961).
17. *Id.* at 297.

behavior or failures to adapt to the requirements of life in society.[18] He concluded that persons facing such problems are responsible for their actions and should be punished if they violate the penal norms of the community. These are his words:

> Not only do I believe that mental illness should never be accepted as a release from criminal responsibility, but also that it should never be the ground for a refusal to try a person charged with an offense. Everyone accused of breaking the law should be tried.[19]

The response to the ideas of Szasz in legal and forensic-psychiatrist circles was largely negative.[20] It was argued that Szasz provided little clinical support for his denial of mental disease, and that he carried the notion of responsibility beyond the limits of its usefulness.

It would indeed be a highly questionable practice to punish persons who are so pervasively disturbed and disordered that they are disabled from making a rational choice between permissible and impermissible conduct. Szasz does not deny that the symptoms to which psychiatrists attach the label "mental disease" exist in reality. He concedes that an individual may commit a homicide because of a genuine complex of persecution or delusional call of religious duty. It would seem that the rationales normally employed to justify punishment are simply not applicable to such situations.

The theory of Szasz may be viewed as an extreme and

---

18. T. SZASZ, LAW, LIBERTY, AND PSYCHIATRY 12-14 (1963); Szasz, *The Sane Slave: Social Control and Legal Psychiatry*, 10 AM. CRIM. L. REV. 337, 349-351, 355 (1972).

19. SZASZ, LAW, LIBERTY, AND PSYCHIATRY, *supra* note 18, at 228. Subsequently Szasz qualified the last sweeping sentence in the quotation by stating that "it might be argued that if a person is in a catatonic state—mute, immobile, and perhaps unable to feed himself—he should not be put on trial," the reason for the exemption being solely the fact that such a person would be unable to assist in his own defense. *Ibid.*

20. See, for example, Schoenfeld, *An Analysis of the Views of Thomas Szasz*, 4 J. PSYCH. & LAW 245 (1976); Dain, Book Review, 3 J. PSYCH. & LAW 381 (1975); Morris, Book Review, 18 U.C.L.A.L. REV. 1164 (1972); Diamond, Book Review, 52 CALIF. L. REV. 899 (1964).

exaggerated reaction to an equally questionable overpsychiatrization of the criminal law. Some authorities in the medical field have taken the position that practically every crime is a sign of mental disorder, which should be cured by treatment rather than punishment.[21] These authorities generally reject the institution of punishment on the ground that psychotic and psychopathic personalities cannot be deterred by the threat of punishment or be resocialized by the application of punishment.

It is difficult to see how the identification of criminality with disease can be made plausible in regard to persons committing economic crimes for the purpose of monetary gain and in the firm expectation of escape from detection. Even systematic acts of violence perpetrated by mafias and other organized gangs lend themselves easily to explanation as a deliberately chosen way of life to insure material success, which might have eluded the members in the legitimate areas of business enterprise. Other offenses for which the application of psychotherapy would hardly seem to be a meaningful alternative to punishment are tax dodging, espionage, reckless driving, and corruption among civil servants.[22]

According to a considerable number of modern studies, even severely disordered personalities are frequently able to respond to threats of punishment or other sanctions.[23] In mental hospitals, for example, habitual compliance by inmates with requirements of proper dress and punctuality at meals, imposed along with announcements of deprivations in case of disobedience, have demonstrated the retention of voluntary controls even by thoroughly psychotic individuals. It is true

---

21. See K. MENNINGER, THE CRIME OF PUNISHMENT (1968); G. ZILBOORG, THE PSYCHOLOGY OF THE CRIMINAL ACT AND PUNISHMENT (1954); H. BARNES & N. TEETERS, NEW HORIZONS IN CRIMINOLOGY 337-338, 817-818 (2d. ed. 1951); H. BARNES, THE STORY OF PUNISHMENT 265-283 (2d ed. 1972).
22. See J. ANDENAES, PUNISHMENT AND DETERRENCE 63-64 (1974).
23. See, for example, W. GLASSER, REALITY THERAPY 107-133 (1965); Wertham, *The Psychiatry of Criminal Guilt*, in THE SOCIAL MEANING OF LEGAL CONCEPTS 164-165 (E. Cahn ed. 1950); Seligman, *Punishment and Voluntary Behavior* (Paper presented at Conference on Rationality and Responsibility, Battelle Seattle Research Center, September 9-12, 1971).

that the possibility of self-control on closely supervised occasions does not in itself prove a corresponding capacity in situations not symbolized by a hospital attendant or policeman at the elbow of the mentally disturbed person.[24] The experiments referred to do suggest, however, that shadings of punishment-responsiveness exist with respect to this category of persons.

D. PROPOSALS TO ABOLISH THE INSANITY DEFENSE

A number of psychiatrists and lawyers have argued that the defense of insanity should be eliminated from criminal proceedings altogether, or at least from that part of the proceedings designed to determine guilt or innocence of the accused person. To the extent that such proposals have originated from Thomas Szasz and those sympathetic to his theories, they are a logical corollary of the view that mental disease is a myth without any basis in fact.[25] But opposition to the insanity plea has also been expressed by authors who believe that the phenomenon known as mental disease does exist. The criminologist Norval Morris, for example, who does not accept the extreme position of Szasz, maintains that the plea of insanity should be interred as anachronistic. In his opinion, evidence of mental illness should be admissible only with respect to the issue whether the accused person had the requisite intent (*mens rea*) necessary for conviction.[26] Seymour Halleck has argued that, since there is no psychiatric agreement on a workable definition of mental disease, the success of an insanity plea often depends merely on the presentation and credentials of the psychiatrists. He believes that those defendants who are wealthy enough to afford a first-class psychiatrist are the ones who chiefly benefit from using the defense.[27]

---

24. See United States v. Brawner, 471 F. 2d 969, 991 (1972).
25. See SZASZ, LAW, LIBERTY, AND PSYCHIATRY, *supra* note 18, at 228-229.
26. Morris, *Psychiatry and the Dangerous Criminal*, 41 SO. CAL. L. REV. 514, 518-519 (1968). Morris would allow "either sane or insane *mens rea* to suffice for guilt." *Id.* at 521.
27. S. HALLECK, PSYCHIATRY AND THE DILEMMAS OF CRIME 215-216 (1967).

The influential English jurist H.L.A. Hart has expressed the view that the insanity defense causes unnecessary confusion for the jury because of vague and conflicting psychiatric evidence. He favors retaining *mens rea* as a necessary element of a crime but not allowing mental abnormality to negate it. This means that the criminal trial would be devoid of psychiatric testimony. Mental disease would be investigated only after conviction and would be primarily concerned with defendant's present rather than his past mental state.[28]

The most radical proposals in this area of the criminal law stem from the pen of Lady Wootton. She advocates not only the elimination of the insanity defense but also the discarding of *mens rea* as a prerequisite of criminal liability. If a person's outward conduct fits the legal definition of a crime, she says, this is sufficient for conviction without proof of a guilty mind. She bases this recommendation on the assumption that we have no reliable criteria by which to distinguish the sick from the healthy mind, so that it becomes impossible to fix the limits of moral and legal responsibility. In her view, the purpose of a criminal trial should consist solely in a finding that a certain offense was committed or not committed by a certain person. The only further question to be determined is that of discerning the most helpful way for preventing such behavior in the future. She holds that this question is to be answered by medical or other experts, who must make every possible effort to reform the offender without reference to any punitive motivation.[29]

The proposals advanced by Lady Wootton contravene the common, one might say almost universal, conviction that a person should not be held guilty of a crime in the absence of some degree of moral blameworthiness. A person who, without a fault of his own, is unaware of the circumstances or possible consequences of his action, or who is so irrational that the restraining force of his superego has become wholly inoperative, should be immune from conviction. Under Lady

---

28. H.L.A. HART, PUNISHMENT AND RESPONSIBILITY 205 (1968); H.L.A. HART, THE MORALITY OF THE CRIMINAL LAW 12-15, 24-25 (1964).
29. B. WOOTTON, SOCIAL SCIENCE AND SOCIAL PATHOLOGY 227-228, 245, 250-252 (1959); B. WOOTTON, CRIME AND THE CRIMINAL LAW 51-81 (1963).

Wootton's theory of strict liability, even a person who commits an offense by pure accident would be criminally liable, although at the dispositional stage of the proceedings such a person would presumably be released.[30]

The more moderate proposal to retain *mens rea* as a general condition of penal liability but to abolish the insanity defense in the context of the criminal trial is also subject to weighty objections. There will be some cases in which the disturbed mental condition of the defendant will negate the presence of *mens rea*, and where the defendant should be acquitted on that ground.[31] If evidence of mental abnormality is excluded from the trial, as Hart proposes, the reason for the denial of *mens rea* and the consequent acquittal will not be clear at the time of the verdict. Since for purposes of ultimate disposition there is a tremendous difference between a plain verdict of acquittal and a verdict of "not guilty by reason of insanity," the ground of acquittal should be brought out in the verdict. The existence or nonexistence of mental disease is too important an element in a criminal proceeding to be withheld from consideration by the jury.[32]

In the majority of cases, a mentally ill defendant will probably have committed the crime with the requisite intent.[33] Even where the defendant was unable to control his emotions or realize the wrongfulness of his act in perpetrating a homicide or assault, this does not mean that he committed the act unconsciously or accidentally rather than willfully. In the

---

30. For a valuable criticism of Lady Wootton's proposals see Kadish, *The Decline of Innocence*, 26 CAMB. L.J. 273, 285-290 (1968).

31. In Sweden, mental condition is relevant at the trial only for the issue of *mens rea*. Defenses based on lack of *mens rea* because of mental disease appear to be rare. Reisner and Semmel, *Abolishing the Insanity Defense: A Look at the Proposed Federal Criminal Code Reform Act in Light of the Swedish Experience*, 62 CALIF. L. REV. 753, 769 (1974).

32. For a criticism of the proposals made by H.L.A. Hart and Lady Wootton see also H. FINGARETTE & A. FINGARETTE HASSE, MENTAL DISABILITIES AND CRIMINAL RESPONSIBILITY 5-6 (1979).

33. "Insanity is quite compatible with intent, moral awareness, and awareness of risk." Gerber, *Is the Insanity Test Insane?*, 20 AM. J. JURIS. 111, 138 (1975). For a valuable and persuasive discussion of the relation between insanity and intent see FINGARETTE & FINGARETTE HASSE, *supra* note 32, at 44-73.

absence of an insanity defense, the jury would have to convict the defendant under these circumstances; his mental condition would become relevant only at a later time when the judge decides whether to commit the defendant to a penal institution or a mental hospital. Since it will be practically impossible to keep the defendant's mental condition entirely out of the perception of the jury, any jury guided by commonsense and fairness would be greatly reluctant to reach a verdict of guilty in the face of obvious delusions or paranoid symptoms. The jury would probably be inclined to acquit the defendant altogether, thereby presumably rendering impossible a court-imposed commitment to a mental hospital.

There are other reasons for holding that an element as crucial for assessing criminal responsibility as the mental condition of the defendant should not be excluded from the trial. In *State v. Strasburg*,[34] the elimination of the insanity defense by the legislature of the state of Washington was held to be a violation of the due process clause of the state constitution and of the right to a jury trial. The court pointed out that the mental responsibility of an accused person was closely related to the determination of guilt, which is entrusted to the jury, and that the decision on this vital issue could not be taken away from the jury. The court also intimated that the question of mental disease was so closely tied in with the problem of *mens rea* that a separate handling of the two matters was highly inappropriate.

The notion that a person should not be convicted of a crime in the absence of blame is deeply entrenched in mankind's collective conscience. If we were forced to adhere to a deterministic philosophy for which the concept of blame is a myth, we might be justified in disregarding the popular sentiment. As was pointed out in the preceding chapter, there are no scientific facts which make it necessary for us to abandon the notion that, as a general rule, human beings have a choice to conform or not to conform to social and legal norms. The insanity defense rests upon the assumption that certain forms of mental disease negate free choice, and that it would be unjust to convict and punish persons who lack the capacity for free choice.

An attempt to incorporate the proposal for abolition of the insanity defense into a proposed revision of the Federal

---

34. 60 Wash. 106, 110 P. 1020 (1910).

Criminal Code[35] was defeated.[36] This idea has also received little favorable response in other countries. It has been pointed out correctly that the abolition proposal overlooks the place which the concept of responsibility plays in keeping the machinery of the criminal law in proper running order.[37]

E. THE LEGAL TESTS OF INSANITY

In psychiatric science, only the central core of the concept of mental disease is well-defined and beyond controversy.[38] This central core includes conditions in which the person in question has lost or almost lost his sense of reality, either with respect to all or with respect to some areas of reality. Outside of this nucleus of consensus, wide disagreement exists among psychiatrists with respect to the criteria by which the existence and nonexistence of mental illness ought to be measured. This psychiatric uncertainty creates grave problems for the administration of criminal justice. It is essential to give some guidance to judges and juries as to what forms of insanity constitute exemptions from criminal liability. As a result, legislatures and courts in many countries of the world have struggled hard with the problem of establishing a legal test of insanity.[39]

For a long period of time, almost all Anglo-American

---
35. S. 1400, 93rd Cong., 1st Sess., §502 (1973).
36. The provision cited *supra* note 35 was omitted from a subsequent version of the bill. See S. 1437, 95th Cong., 2d Sess. (1978).
37. A. GOLDSTEIN, THE INSANITY DEFENSE 223 (1967). See also Kadish, *supra* note 30, at 282-285, and G. FLETCHER, RETHINKING CRIMINAL LAW 843-846 (1978).
38. Waelder, *Psychiatry and the Problem of Criminal Responsibility*, 101 U. PA. L. REV. 378, 384 (1952); Diamond, *From Durham to Brawner: A Futile Journey*, 1973 WASH. U.L. QU. 109, 115; Halleck, *supra* note 27, at 216.
39. An attempt was made by the United States Court of Appeals for the District of Columbia to dispense with a legal definition of mental disease and leave the determination of the impact of mental disease upon criminal responsibility to the psychiatric experts. Durham v. United States, 214 F.2d 862 (1954). The experiment was a failure and was soon abandoned. See McDonald v. United States, 312 F.2d 847, 850-851 (1962); United States v. Brawner, 471 F.2d 969, 976-984 (1972).

jurisdictions found the criterion of legal insanity in the well-known *M'Naghten* rule. Under this rule, the jury is asked to determine whether the actor by reason of mental disease or defect did not know the nature or quality of his act, or did not know that it was wrong. This was a minimalist test of insanity, which was objected to by most psychiatrists and many lawyers on the ground that it placed an undue emphasis on the purely intellectual and cognitive aspects of mental disease. Even high-grade psychotics rarely suffer from a major impairment of their cognitive faculties. It was pointed out that many forms of mental disturbance show symptoms of a volitive-emotional nature which destroy, at least in the most severe cases, the actor's capacity to conform his conduct to the requirements of the law.[40]

A minority of jurisdictions recognized a further ground of exculpation if the actor's conduct was the result of an "irresistible impulse." Under this test, a defendant in a criminal case will be acquitted if, as a result of mental disease, he was totally deprived of will power to resist the criminal impulse, although he knew that his act was wrong. This test has often been criticized as being too narrow. It appears to confine the defense of insanity to acts which were committed under a sudden and impulsive surge of emotion. It is possible that a criminal act may have been cooly and carefully prepared and yet be the deed of a madman who has lost his sense of reality.[41]

The American Model Penal Code has adopted a test of insanity which is broader in scope than the two aforementioned criteria. The test was formulated as follows:

> (1) A person is not responsible for criminal conduct if at the time of such conduct as a result of mental disease or defect he lacks substantial capacity either to appreciate the criminality [wrongfulness] of his conduct or to conform his conduct to the requirements of law.

---

40. See LAFAVE & SCOTT, *supra* note 13, at 280-281. If the *M'Naghten* rule is strictly construed, it will cover only the case of an individual in an extreme state of stuporous catatonic schizophrenia, and the case of a raving maniac or imbecile. United States v. Currens, 290 F.2d 751, 774, note 32 (1961).
41. LAFAVE & SCOTT, *supra* note 13, at 283-286.

(2) As used in this Article, the terms "mental disease or defect" do not include an abnormality manifested only by repeated criminal or otherwise anti-social conduct.[42]

In recent years, this test was adopted by the federal courts of the United States and a number of states of the Union.[43] The largest state of the Union, California, accepted the test in 1978, after a long, unbroken adherence to the *M'Naghten* rule.[44] Most of the draft codes now pending in other states have proposed this standard for legislative enactment. The Model Code test is also recognized as the most appropriate legal criterion of mental disease in a large number of countries throughout the world.[45]

The Model Code approach avoids the implication contained in the irresistible impulse test that loss of the actor's control functions can be reflected only in sudden and spontaneous acts, as distinguished from those accompanied by brooding and deliberation. It excludes, on the other hand, from the concept of mental disease those psychopathic offenders who suffer from an underdeveloped social conscience without showing the marks of a disease which destroys the possibility of rational behavior. This is a judicious compromise which has a good chance of further wide acceptance in the future.

Although the second paragraph of the Model Code provision is designed to guard against an undue extension of the legal insanity concept, the success of this solution depends to a large extent upon the attitude of the psychiatric profession. A forensic psychiatrist committed to a strictly deterministic philosophy might in the majority of cases involving the insanity defense take the position that the accused person was unable to prevent himself from committing the offense. If this

---

42. MODEL PENAL CODE §4.01 (Proposed Official Draft 1962).
43. See Wechsler, *The Model Penal Code and the Codification of American Criminal Law*, in CRIME, CRIMINOLOGY AND PUBLIC POLICY 441-446 (R. Hood ed. 1974).
44. People v. Drew, 22 Cal. 3rd 333, 149 Cal. Rptr. 275, 583 P.2d 1318 (1978).
45. Information obtained by the writer from the Max-Planck-Institute for Foreign and International Criminal Law at Freiburg (West Germany).

position is widely accepted by judges and juries, it might lead to an overuse of the insanity defense, at least in cases carrying severe penalties, and a consequent overtaxing of public mental hospital facilities.

To obviate this danger as much as possible, the jury should be instructed that the law raises a strong factual presumption of free will and responsibility. This presumption can be overcome only by highly persuasive evidence to the effect that the defendant was deprived of rationality to such an extent that he had no power to avoid doing what he did.[46] If it can be concluded by a court or jury in a particular case that an evisceration of the rational control functions has occurred, so that the offender has become a playball of irrational forces, then responsibility should be denied and the insanity plea upheld.

Even for a psychiatrist who does not accept a radically deterministic philosophy it will sometimes be hard to draw a line between persons able and unable to control their actions. For this reason a leading penologist, Professor Johannes Andenaes, has proposed the following modification of the Model Code test: A person is not responsible for criminal conduct if at the time of such conduct, as a result of mental disease or defect, his capacity to appreciate the criminality of his conduct or to conform his conduct to the requirements of the law is so substantially impaired that he cannot justly be held responsible.[47] The advantage of this formula lies in its flexibility. It permits the psychiatric experts and jury to infer from a thorough appraisal of the defendant's personality and behavior whether or not the processes of the criminal law are the appropriate means for dealing with his offense and for influencing his future conduct. It needs to be recognized, however, that the present text of the Model Code provision also contains language which imparts a certain degree of open-endedness to the administration of the test: the loss of the

---

46. For a definition of insanity which makes the inability to act rationally the touchstone of mental disease see H. FINGARETTE, THE MEANING OF CRIMINAL INSANITY 211 (1972). See also the more recent discussion of the nature of legal insanity in FINGARETTE & FINGARETTE HASSE, *supra* note 32, at 38-40, 206-211.

47. Statement of Professor Johannes Andenaes at the hearing before the Senate Subcommittee on Criminal Laws and Procedures, *supra* note 2, at 2955.

defendant's control powers need not be total but only "substantial."

F. DIMINISHED RESPONSIBILITY

The notion of diminished responsibility was introduced in England by the Homicide Act of 1957.[48] A defendant accused of murder is permitted to raise the defense that he was suffering from an abnormality of mind which substantially reduces his responsibility. Abnormality of mind was defined by a court to mean a state of mind so different from that of ordinary human beings that a reasonable man would term it abnormal.[49] If the defense is successful, the jury may convict the defendant of manslaughter rather than murder. The trial judge is given discretion either to order the imprisonment of the defendant or to commit him or her to a mental hospital.[50]

A number of states in the United States followed suit, without uniformly copying the exact British model. Particularly instructive is the experience of California, which introduced the defense under the label "diminished capacity." As in England, the doctrine is used to reduce an accusation of premeditated murder to a lesser charge (which may be either second-degree murder or manslaughter), but it is not necessarily confined to this situation. It is to be noted that in California the issues of guilt and mental disease are adjudged separately in two distinct phases of the trial. Evidence of mental disorder may be introduced at the first phase only to show that the defendant, because of his mental condition, did not possess the specific intent required by the statutory definition of the crime.[51]

In *People v. Wells*,[52] the defendant was charged with assaulting a prison guard with malice aforethought, a capital offense. The defendant offered evidence that he had been

---

48. 5 & 6 Eliz. 2, c. 2, §2; 8 HALSBURY'S STATUTES OF ENGLAND 459 (3rd ed. 1969).
49. Rex v. Byrne, [1960] 3 All. E.R. 1, 4-5.
50. 11 HALSBURY'S LAWS OF ENGLAND, Sec. 546 (4th ed. 1976).
51. See Louisell & Hazard, *Insanity as a Defense: The Bifurcated Trial*, 49 CALIF. L. REV. 805, 818 (1961).
52. 33 Cal.2d 330, 202 P.2d 53 (1949).

suffering from nervous tensions which made him abnormally susceptible of fearing for his life. The evidence was excluded by the trial court, but this ruling was found to be in error by the California Supreme Court. The court held that malice aforethought was a specific element of the crime charged, which the prosecution must prove beyond a reasonable doubt. A defendant may therefore introduce psychiatric testimony regarding his state of mind at the first phase of his trial, which is designed to raise the question of his capacity to harbor malice. In the end result, however, the lower court's error was held not to be ground for reversal because there was substantial evidence supporting the finding of malice.

In *People v. Gorshen*,[53] the defendant, in front of a number of witnesses including several police officers, shot and killed the foreman of the company for which he worked. Earlier on the same day, he had had an altercation with the foreman, in the course of which he was knocked down by him and slightly injured. Gorshen had been drinking heavily before this event took place. He told several people he was going home to get a gun, which he did; he returned after a while and committed the murder. The case looks like a typical example of premeditated murder, yet Gorshen was convicted of second-degree murder on the basis of testimony by a forensic psychiatrist that Gorshen was mentally abnormal and therefore incapable to premeditate and entertain malice. The expert expressed the view that the deed was the product of unconscious forces rather than of the actor's free will.

In a number of later cases, too, the California Supreme Court reduced a charge of first-degree murder to a lesser degree in situations where a homicide had been committed after careful preparations.[54] The justification for such decisions becomes especially questionable where conviction for the crime is reduced to manslaughter, an offense which the defendant never

---

53. 51 Cal.2d 716, 336 P.2d 492 (1959).
54. See, for example, People v. Wolff, 61 Cal. 2d 795, 40 Cal. Rptr. 271, 394 P.2d 959 (1964); People v. Conley, 64 Cal.2d 310, 49 Cal. Rptr. 815, 411 P.2d 911 (1966); People v. Goedecke, 65 Cal.2d 850, 56 Cal. Rptr. 625, 423 P.2d 777 (1967); People v. Poddar, 10 Cal.3rd 750, 111 Cal. Rptr. 910, 518 P.2d 342 (1974).

committed. The case of *People v. Conley*[55] may serve as an example. Conley had killed his former girl friend and her husband, three days after she had ended their affair. On the day of the shooting, he bought a rifle, practiced shooting, and told his friends that he was going to kill the couple. Conley relied on the defense of diminished capacity, showing that he had been drinking heavily before committing the crime. The jury convicted Conley of first-degree murder. The California Supreme Court reversed, holding that the lower court had erred in not giving the requested instructions on voluntary manslaughter.

Voluntary manslaughter is killing upon a sudden quarrel or heat of passion.[56] These requirements were not fulfilled in *Conley*, since the deed had been carefully prepared. In the opinion of the Supreme Court, the jury should have been advised that defendant's diminished capacity, due to his intoxication, could have prevented him from harboring the "malice aforethought" necessary for murder. It is true that under the California Penal Code intoxication may be shown to negate an essential state of mind.[57] It is highly doubtful whether intoxication, as a matter of policy, should be considered a defense to a charge of murder, especially if the defendant put himself in a state of drunkenness to remove inhibitions to the commission of the crime. Regardless of the answer to this question, it is difficult to accept the ruling of the court that the lower court should have instructed the jury on voluntary manslaughter.

If in cases of diminished capacity the degree of the homicide is reduced to manslaughter, the defendant may get away with a relatively short prison term, although the social dangerousness of the person, because of the weakness of his internal controls, may be particularly great.[58] Although from the point of view of

---

55. *Supra* note 54.
56. Cal. Penal Code §192.
57. Cal. Penal Code §22. A useful discussion of the defense of intoxication is found in FINGARETTE & FINGARETTE HASSE, *supra* note 32, at 77-104, and G. FLETCHER, *supra* note 37, at 846-852.
58. If the charge is reduced to manslaughter, conviction will result in imprisonment for two, three, or four years. Cal. Penal Code §193. See in this connection Arenella, *The Diminished Capacity and*

justice for the individual it is fair to adjust the severity of the penalty to the degree of the accused person's culpability, the penological rationale of protecting society from individuals who have deepseated difficulties in conforming their conduct to the requirements of the law must also receive strong consideration. Furthermore, where a crime, unlike homicide, is not gradated into various shadings of seriousness, a finding that a defendant, because of diminished capacity, was unable to form the requisite criminal intent may result in the defendant's complete acquittal. Because of these unquestionable difficulties, it is possible that the California Supreme Court may someday modify its approach to diminished capacity. There is reason to believe that the doctrine was adopted initially to mitigate the rigidity of the *M'Naghten* rule. This rule, as has been mentioned, was replaced by the Model Code test in 1978.[59] The conditions under which the California Supreme Court has in the past recognized the diminished capacity test would probably meet the requirements of insanity under the Model Code test in a considerable number of cases. In these cases, the defendant may have been aware of the wrongfulness of his conduct, but because of mental disease may have been unable to conform his conduct to the requirements of the law.

The diminished capacity defense would under these circumstances be limited to cases in which the accused, though not legally insane, had suffered a diminution of his volitional control functions. Under the West German Criminal Code, the court in such cases may impose a lesser punishment; but it may in its discretion refuse to do so if the social dangerousness of the defendant demands a long-term imprisonment notwithstanding the impaired voluntariness of his actions.[60] This solution recommends itself as reasonable, because it affords the public a better potential protection than the present practice of the California Supreme Court to reduce, in homicide cases, a charge of first-degree murder to a lesser degree of the crime.[61]

Diminished Responsibility Defenses, 77 COLUM. L. REV. 827, 850, 853 (1977) and Dix, *Psychological Abnormality as a Factor in Grading Liability: Diminished Capacity, Diminished Responsibility, and the Like,* 62 J. CRIM. L., CRIMIN. & POL. SCI. 313, 322 (1971).

59. People v. Drew, *supra* note 44.
60. German Criminal Code, *supra* note 12, §35.
61. Under California's determinate sentence law, the judge usually

G. CONCLUSION

Justice Cardozo made the following statement in *Steward Machine Company v. Davis*: "Till now the law has been guided by a robust common sense which assumes the freedom of the will as a working hypothesis in the solution of its problems."[62] The attempt has been made in the preceding chapter to demonstrate that the evidence gathered in the sciences does not compel us to discard this working hypothesis of free will. This means that the criminal law is justified in adhering to a strong presumption of sanity, which can be overcome only by convincing proof tending to show lack of personal responsibility.

An acceptance of this position would restore the concept of responsibility to its proper place in the social and legal order.[63] A wholesale denial of responsibility is not only unsupported by scientific evidence, as is being realized to an increasing extent throughout the world. A denial of responsibility also has deleterious psychological consequences: to tell people that they have no power over their actions tends to prevent or weaken efforts to build inner controls. Individuals should be considered responsible for their conduct unless their decisional freedom has been destroyed or gravely impaired by a severe form of mental illness. This approach reflects the sentiments of justice of the average person without offending the findings of scientific truth.

---

has a choice between a normal, an aggravated, and a mitigated prison term. Whether or not additional legislation would be required, especially in homicide cases, to implement the solution here proposed for the diminished capacity (preferably: diminished responsibility) problem need not be discussed here. A valuable discussion of the attitude of the California Supreme Court towards the problem of diminished capacity is found in FINGARETTE & FINGARETTE HASSE, *supra* note 32, at 117-133.

62. 301 U.S. 548, 590 (1937).

63. See in this connection FINGARETTE & FINGARETTE HASSE, *supra* note 32, at 11: "The problems are ripe for a return to the basic common law principles centering around the notion of responsibility, which lies at the heart of the criminal law in all common law lands."

PART II

The Varieties of Responsibility

CHAPTER 4

Existential Responsibility

A. FOUNDATIONS OF EXISTENTIAL RESPONSIBILITY

The thesis was put forward in Chapter 1 that human beings have responsibilities toward themselves. The recognition of such responsibilities is rooted in the fact that each individual has a potential for achievement which he cannot attain without substantial self-direction and effort on his part. If he neglects to make this effort, preferring to vegetate, drift, and malinger, he is likely to experience regrets at some time in his life that he has wasted his innate gifts and missed out on his opportunities. Since his parasitic style of life will earn him little respect and concern from his fellowmen, he will suffer additional pain on this account. Furthermore, it is natural for every individual to project in his mind an image of what he would like to become, and he will not enjoy inner peace and harmony unless he makes a strong attempt to convert this image into reality. It is reasonable to hold, in light of these considerations, that the present ego owes an obligation to the future, more complete, ego to move on toward actualization of what the individual is capable of becoming. Existential responsibility may be expressed in the following categorical imperative: "Endeavor to reach the highest level of human existence which you are able to attain in view of your individual capabilities."

There are three layers of human existence to which

existential responsibility must relate itself. The first layer consists of those traits, drives, and needs which are common to human beings generally. The second layer comprises those features of character which are not universal attributes of the human race but which are possessed by certain types of individuals. The third one includes the special endowments, aptitudes, and other components of personality which, in their peculiar combination and interrelation, make an individual a unique and singular member of the human race.

B. RESPONSIBILITY AND COMMON HUMAN TRAITS

There are some traits which human beings share with all of their fellowmen. Among the strongest and most pervasive of these traits are the urge for food and the sex drive. Both of them stem from basic needs of the human organism.

These drives operate in a self-initiating and more or less automatic manner. They require no stimulus from the outside; the human organism takes care that they are experienced as tangible realities of human existence. The problem of responsibility arises, therefore, not so much as an obligation to foster or strengthen these drives, but primarily as a set of efforts to curb extreme or deleterious modes of their gratification. If the drive for food gets out of control, this may create health hazards caused by gluttony or obesity. An insatiable concentration on the sex drive may, over prolonged periods of time, result in premature aging or a withdrawal of energy from important life tasks.[1]

All human beings also have a need for safety, which is closely related to the instinct of self-preservation. The need for secure conditions of life is particularly strong in the child who, in Maslow's words, "seems to want a predictable, lawful, orderly world."[2] The child's preference for a structured environment is a concomitant of his dependence on others, particularly his parents, which makes a regular and reliable attendance to his needs essential for his wellbeing.

---

1. For a discussion of the relation between biological drives and cultural growth see *infra* Chapter 8 (C and D).
2. A. MASLOW, MOTIVATION AND PERSONALITY 40 (2d ed. 1970).

The desire for safety persists, in an attenuated form, in adulthood. Human beings wish to be protected from the vicissitudes of weather, danger of accidents, criminal assault, murder, and other hazards. Here again, the principle of responsibility serves primarily to ward off unwholesome manifestations of the drive, rather than to support the drive as such. There is no doubt that an inordinate degree of insecurity is not conducive to personality growth, because a state of constant or prolonged apprehension tends to cripple initiative and productive work. On the other hand, as Gordon Allport has pointed out, a certain amount of personal, social, and economic insecurity may be beneficial to individual development.[3] Risk, adventure, and exploration of the unknown may infuse vitality into the personality and strengthen such qualities as courage, fortitude and resourcefulness. The responsible individual will therefore do whatever lies in his power to procure for himself conditions of life in which he can conduct his activities in a state of mental equilibrium, while at the same time he will have to prepare himself for enduring dangers and hazards without losing his stamina.

Another universal trait of human beings is the quest for recognition and esteem by their fellowmen.[4] People wish to receive high evaluations from others and to enjoy a good reputation. An individual who does the best he can to be of service to his society will normally (though not necessarily) gain the appreciation he seeks from others and thereby strengthen his own self-esteem. What he must avoid is to overextend the need for esteem into an unbounded ambition and craze for prestige, with the possible consequence that means may be used for the enhancement of individual power which society is unwilling to tolerate. History is full of examples in which an excessive greed for power resulted in ultimate defeat for the power-seeker.

Individuals also have a wish to be loved, which is clearly distinguishable from the sexual instinct. This common trait of human beings manifests itself in a longing for the emotional acceptance of one's whole personality by others, who may be of the same or the opposite sex. This urge, like the closely-related

---
3. G. ALLPORT, PERSONALITY AND SOCIAL ENCOUNTER 353 (1960).
4. See MASLOW, *supra* note 2, at 45-46.

esteem need, is healthy if it does not transcend the proper bounds. Some persons simply do not have a lovable personality, and their emotional needs will be gratified, if at all, only by very few of their fellow human beings. Such persons may have to overcompensate their desire for love by socially valuable accomplishments. It is well known, for example, that Ludwig van Beethoven was an unattractive, awkward, discourteous man unable to gain the affection he sought, especially from members of the female sex. The responsibility he felt toward his calling as a composer prevented him from turning into a pathological, frustrated individual incapable of performing the great tasks which destiny had assigned to him.

The common human traits thus far discussed—the food-seeking drive, the sex drive, the quest for safety, the desire for esteem, and the wish to be loved—are not in need of external encouragement because they are self-propelling impulses of the human personality. There is another common trait which must receive a somewhat different treatment. "All men by nature desire to know," said Aristotle.[5] St. Thomas Aquinas agreed with him,[6] and a number of modern psychologists have accepted this view.[7] Indeed, children of normal intellect are curious about the world around them, ask many questions about it, and seek to explore it whenever an opportunity presents itself. The normal adult retains this quest for knowledge, but it cannot be said that the wish to learn operates as spontaneously and quasi-automatically as the physiological and emotional drives of human beings. If the desire to increase one's knowledge receives no encouragement and support from the environment, it can become smothered and even extinguished. Man can suppress his intellect and live a pure life of the body and emotions, although such a mode of life is likely to be hurtful to him in the long run. A responsible individual will make every attempt to enhance and deepen his knowledge,

---

5. Aristotle, *Metaphysics*, in THE BASIC WORKS OF ARISTOTLE 689 (R. McKeon ed. 1941).
6. ST. THOMAS AQUINAS, SUMMA THEOLOGICA, Pt. II, 1st pt., Qu. 94, Art. 2 (Fathers of the English Dominican Province transl. 1913-1925).
7. E. FROMM, MAN BY HIMSELF 46-47, 102-106 (1947); P. SCHILDER, GOALS AND DESIRES OF MEN 220 (1942); MASLOW, *supra* note 2, at 48-51; G. ALLPORT, BECOMING 51-54 (1955).

because this will give him some measure of control over the conditions surrounding him and enable him to cope with the more complex contingencies of life. It is justifiable under these circumstances that the State compels young people by law to go to school and receive an education.

One might ponder the reasons why human impulses relating to the mind and intellect are in need of external reinforcement, while this is not true for the biological and emotional drives. The most convincing answer is that the latter drives are stronger, more elementary, and self-operating, while thinking and reason are tender plants which require a great deal of care and nurturing to develop properly.

C. RESPONSIBILITY AND INDIVIDUAL TRAITS

There are traits of human beings which are not descriptive of the human race as such, but are possessed only by certain types of persons. Some of the traits in this second category are generally viewed as beneficial and desirable, while others are considered detrimental to a healthy individual and social life.

From the angle of responsibility, little needs to be said about those human qualities which classical philosophy has denominated "virtues." Examples are benevolence, tolerance, generosity, courage, honesty, and reliability. They ought to be fostered by the individual and encouraged by society in the educational process.

There are other personality traits which adversely affect the growth of an individual and inhibit his contributions to the well-being of society. The only ones which will be discussed here are violent aggressiveness and addiction to certain substances which enable individuals to escape from the harshnesses of reality, such as alcohol and drugs.

There is no need to ventilate the much-discussed question whether the propensity for aggression is an innate or acquired characteristic of human beings. Hobbes and Freud believed that the desire to hurt was endemic to the human race.[8] Today, there

---

8. T. HOBBES, DE CIVE, Pt. I, Ch. 1.3-4 (S. Lamprecht ed. 1949); S.

is a growing consensus to the effect that this view represents an overbroad generalization.[9] There are, to be sure, persons born with a violent disposition who, if they can be held back at all from committing aggressive acts, can be curbed only by the power of the law. Most people do not exhibit traits of malignant aggressiveness, but some will develop them if they are mistreated by their fellowmen or seriously frustrated in their life aims. If such frustration turns into psychotic illness, the responsibility of the afflicted individuals for acts harmful to others may erode. In other cases, it may become diminished by emotional pressures difficult to resist.[10] Under ordinary circumstances, however, a person will be able to keep his antisocial impulses in check, not only because of external threats of punishment, but also by utilizing his internal controls.

Some people are unable, by predisposition, acquired habits, or unfortunate experiences, to resist the temptations offered by the consumption of psychedelic drugs, alcohol, and tobacco. As long as moderate quantities of use are involved, no serious threat to health may ensue. Addictive use is, however, an everpresent danger and may have far-reaching consequences for the individual and those close to him. A responsible individual will consider it his obligation to care about his health in order to lead a productive life and avoid future suffering by him and others.

A different approach to the problem was taken by Samuel Shuman, who has argued from a position of extreme liberalism that everybody has a right to be unhealthy.[11] He asserts that this

---

FREUD, CIVILIZATION AND ITS DISCONTENTS 58-61 (J. Strachey transl. 1961).

9. E. FROMM, THE ANATOMY OF HUMAN DESTRUCTIVENESS 218-267, 435-478 (1973); M. ASHLEY MONTAGUE, ON BEING HUMAN 43-45, 92-95 (1951); V. FRANKL, AGGRESSION AND EXISTENTIAL FRUSTRATION (Lecture, University of Navarra, 1976); B. MALINOWSKI, FREEDOM AND CIVILIZATION 276-280 (1944). Konrad Lorenz, who assumed a human instinct of aggression, expressed optimism concerning the possibility of controlling destructive aggressiveness. ON AGGRESSION 275-299 (M. Wilson transl. 1963).

10. See the discussion of diminished responsibility *supra* Chapter 3 (F).

11. Shuman, *The Right to be Unhealthy*, 22 WAYNE L. REV. 61 (1975).

right has always been in jeopardy, but that the danger has been increased by "medical expansionism and imperialism" and abetted by governmental welfare services. He believes that the social pressure for health is related to the crime problem and in part caused by the "primitive" belief that crime is a function of abnormality, so that increased health (obviously meaning mental health) will reduce crime. In his opinion, however, we should have learned the lesson in the twentieth century "that it is entirely possible that only the 'healthiest' will commit what at a certain time and place is defined as a (statutory) crime."[12]

Underlying any justification of medieval imperialism, Shuman says, is the assumption that diseases are biophysical realities which are not invented by doctors but are "out there" waiting to be discovered. Shuman is convinced that behind this assumption lies a particularly tenacious, but pernicious, form of the myth about the value neutrality of science, a myth which mistakes theories for facts.[13] According to Shuman, "a disease is an attribution and not a description."[14]

Shuman outlines certain conditions—which are fairly narrowly delimited—under which he would allow the right to be unhealthy to be "compromised" by therapeutic intervention.[15] But his doubts regarding the possibility of distinguishing clearly between health and disease drive him to the final conclusion that "we may be forced to accept health anarchy— not because it is so good, but because no more attractive alternative is available."[16]

The position of Shuman is unsound and should be rejected. It is in the interest of every individual to keep and improve his health because this is an indispensable condition for leading a satisfactory life. Furthermore, society must be concerned about the health of its members if it wishes to remain a going concern and keep its productive capacity on a high level. These considerations necessitate the adoption of a philosophy which will instill in individuals, at an early period of their lives, a sense of responsibility for their healthful growth, instead of

---

12. *Id.* at 63.
13. *Id.* at 63-64.
14. *Id.* at 79.
15. *Id.* at 81-82.
16. *Id.* at 85.

telling them that, subject to certain exceptions, they have a right to be unhealthy.

The view of Shuman that a medical diagnosis of disease rests on theory rather than fact is also untenable in its generality. There are, of course, many situations where doubt exists with respect to the existence of a certain disease. In the large majority of cases, however, all members of the medical profession will agree that the patient has contracted a certain illness as a matter of fact rather than "attribution." It should not be necessary in the world of academia to belabor the obvious.

Shuman is afraid that society may in a paternalistic manner force upon individuals certain therapies believed to improve their health. This apprehension may be justified if, for example, inmates of prisons or mental hospitals are compelled to undergo dangerous operations, such as lobotomy, which may remove certain conditions responsible for abnormal or criminal behavior but which will at the same time destroy vital cognitive or emotional functions. On the other hand, the legally authorized administration of drugs which help people to overcome states of high tension, or which may curb aggressive behavior, are not deserving of censure if proper safeguards against abuse are provided. The same is true of reasonable therapeutic measures designed to counteract alcoholism or drug addiction.

Shuman is right when he argues that criminality is not necessarily a sign of disease.[17] He overshoots his mark, however, when he asserts that criminal behavior is often a sign of health. The commission of crimes for the most part evinces a socially unhealthy condition of the mind. While medical measures may be inappropriate in curing a sociopathic attitude, a social-educative treatment of the criminal may be helpful in changing his mental outlook. What is needed more than anything else is to imbue in the offender a sense of responsibility vis-a-vis the basic values of community living.

D. RESPONSIBILITY FOR SELF-PERFECTION

The question whether or not human beings have an innate drive for self-perfection has been the subject of

---
17. See *supra* Chapter 3 (C).

controversy. Freud did not believe in the existence of such an inner impulse. "The development of man up to now," he said, "does not seem to me to need any explanation differing from that of animal development, and the restless striving towards further perfection which may be observed in a minority of human beings is easily explicable as a result of that repression of instinct upon which what is most valuable in culture is built."[18] He was convinced that the inclinations of ordinary persons tend toward the maintenance of an inner equilibrium and the reduction of nervous tensions, rather than toward a restless, tension-producing urge to reach out into the higher, spiritual levels of energy.[19] Alfred Adler maintained, on the other hand, that a striving for perfection accompanied each individual throughout his life, beginning in early childhood in the form of an innate disposition. "The key to the entire social process is to be found in the fact that persons are always striving to find a situation in which they can excel."[20] He was certain that persons lacking the "upward" drive were bound to lead unhappy and frustrated lives.

Humanistic psychology in the twentieth century has given support to the view of Adler. Erich Fromm declares that "all men are 'idealists' and are striving for something beyond the attainment of physical satisfaction."[21] If the individual faces the truth without panic, he says, he will recognize that there is no meaning to life except the meaning which man gives his existence by the unfolding of his powers, by living productively.[22] Abraham Maslow states that human life will never be understood unless its highest aspirations are taken into account. "Growth, self-actualization, the striving toward health, the quest for identity and autonomy, the yearning for excellence (and other ways of phrasing the striving 'upward') must by now be accepted beyond question as a widespread and

---

18. Freud, *Beyond the Pleasure Principle,* in THE MAJOR WORKS OF SIGMUND FREUD 654 (Great Books of the Western World v. 54, R. Hutchins ed. 1952).
19. *Id.* at 639-640.
20. A. ADLER, THE SCIENCE OF LIVING 74 (1929).
21. FROMM, *supra* note 7, at 49.
22. *Id.* at 45.

perhaps universal human tendency."[23] Viktor Frankl and Gordon Allport have taken the same position.[24]

There is no need to undertake an exploration of the question whether or not the striving for self-perfection is or is not inborn in human beings. Even if it is an ingredient of human nature, the will to excel may be counteracted and frustrated by a tendency toward inertia, sloth, and indolence which also forms part of the human makeup. Few people would argue that the trend toward reduction of effort should be given preference by society over the desire for accomplishment. Innumerable productive individuals throughout history have testified to the deep inner satisfaction which is derived from creativity and achievement. Even those who seek nothing in life except instant pleasure would feel quite uncomfortable in a human world dominated by the animal instincts and incapable of providing the amenities of civilization, which can be secured only by inventiveness and hard work.

If there is agreement that the fullest possible unfolding of all human capabilities is eminently desirable, then it becomes the responsibility of every individual to strive toward the goal of self-improvement. The discharge of this responsibility will require the overcoming of inertia, as well as some channeling and control of the purely libidinous energies.[25] It will also necessitate the fostering of habits of study and work, an acquisition of knowledge essential to a rounded development of the personality, and a substantial investment of energy and effort in occupational pursuits.

The process of self-actualization will bring out the existential potentialities latent in the individual. Some of these potentialities will consist in a peculiar, highly individualized combination of gifts and abilities. In the words of Frankl, there is "an implicit summons to men to actualize in their own lives their unique and singular possibilities."[26] But the effort at self-improvement must also be concerned with developing those

---

23. MASLOW, *supra* note 2, at xii-xiii.
24. V. FRANKL, THE WILL TO MEANING 38 (1969); ALLPORT, *supra* note 7, at 47-51.
25. See *infra* Chapter 8 (C and D).
26. V. FRANKL, THE DOCTOR AND THE SOUL 44 (1967).

common human qualities which are conducive to genuine accomplishment in life.

The desire of the individual to reach his highest potential can and should receive some psychological reinforcement from the outside world. If, in our treatment of young people, we convey to them, explicitly or implicitly, our expectation and belief that they are capable of making an impact in some field of endeavor, we thereby strengthen their self-respect and forward drive. In consonance with this pedagogical principle, the German poet Goethe is reported to have expressed the following thought in a conversation: "If we treat people as they are, we make them worse. If we treat them as if they were what they ought to be, we help them to become what they are capable of becoming."[27]

E. EGOTISM AND ALTRUISM

This writer agrees with Roberto Unger that personality has two aspects: "one universal, represented by sociability and the abstract self; the other particular, expressed by individuality and the concrete self."[28] This chapter has dealt with the responsibilities which an individual should display toward his concrete self, for the purpose of developing a well-rounded personality capable of coping with the manifold tasks of life. The chapters that follow will treat the other-regarding facets of responsibility. Implicit in this approach is the assumption that responsibility centered on the ego can be combined and harmonized with responsible attitudes directed toward others.

There are writers who deny that a complementary relation can or should exist between egotistic and altruistic behavior. The advocacy of a radical form of egotism by Max Stirner has already been mentioned.[29] "I am owner of humanity, am humanity, and do nothing for the good of another humanity. Fool, you who are a unique humanity, that you make a merit of wanting to live for another than you are."[30]

---

27. Quoted by FRANKL, *supra* note 26, at 7.
28. R. UNGER, KNOWLEDGE AND POLITICS 239 (1975).
29. See *supra* Chapter 1 (C).
30. M. STIRNER, THE EGO AND HIS OWN 245 (S. Byington transl. 1963).

More recently, Ayn Rand has proclaimed selfishness as a supreme virtue. In her opinion, the ethical purpose of every individual is his own life: "This basic *social* principle of the Objectivist ethics is that just as life is an end in itself, so every living human being is an end in himself, not the means to the ends or the welfare of others—and therefore, that man must live for his own sake, neither sacrificing himself to others nor sacrificing others to himself."[31]

Ayn Rand argues that, if civilization is to survive, it is the altruist morality that men have to reject.[32] She defines altruism as the view which declares that "any action taken for the benefit of others is good, and any action taken for one's own benefit is evil."[33] She also asserts that "altruism permits no concept of a self-respecting, self-supporting man—a man who supports his life by his own effort and neither sacrifices himself nor others."[34]

Ayn Rand's conception of altruism presupposes an irreconcilable conflict between egotistic and altruistic motivations. This assumption cannot be accepted. Altruism does not assert that "any action taken for one's own benefit is evil," nor does it reject the notion of a self-respecting, self-supporting person. Altruism holds that actions done by an individual for the benefit of other individuals are desirable and laudable, even though such actions may not be compatible in a particular situation with the purely self-serving concerns of an individual. Altruism does not hold that an individual should forego acting in support of his own life and interests. It is sympathetic to the value of self-esteem but teaches that a person's self-respect may be enhanced by selfless conduct. Contrary to the view of Ayn Rand, the altruistic philosophy maintains that self-sacrifice in the interest of transpersonal values may be admirable. It assumes that the world would be a poorer place to live in if personalities like Socrates and Jesus had never existed.

---

31. A. RAND, THE VIRTUE OF SELFISHNESS 22-23 (1964). See also *id.* at 19, where she states that the ethical purpose of every person is his own life.
32. *Id.* at 34.
33. *Id.* at x.
34. *Id.* at xii.

While Ayn Rand concedes the possibility of altruistic actions, a recent popular book on the subject declares bluntly that "there is no such thing as altruism."[35] According to the thesis of the book's author, there exist only rational and irrational selfishness. Mahatma Gandhi was acting selfishly when he sacrificed himself for the freedom of the Indian people; this was the way he chose to seek his own happiness.[36]

Such denial of the very possibility of altruistic motivation is unconvincing. A woman who foregoes a much-desired trip abroad with her husband in order to stay close to her old ailing mother, in case an emergency should arise, makes a decision contrary to her egoistic interest. The fact that she may derive some inner satisfaction from her decision would appear to be a minor element in a situation which clearly involves an act of unselfishness and self-sacrifice. Similar considerations apply to the case of a martyr. He, too, may derive some deep satisfaction from his actions; but the fact that he is willing to suffer pain and even death for the sake of a political, social, or religious cause places him at the opposite pole from an individual who will never do anything that would interfere with his personal comfort and pleasurable pursuits.

There are, to be sure, many human actions that represent a blend between self-regarding and other-regarding motivations. There are others that can be clearly classified as either egoistic or altruistic. Most people will on some occasions act selfishly, on others unselfishly, and in many cases perform actions out of mixed motives. It has been argued that the drawing of a sharp line of demarcation between egotism and altruism is for this and other reasons unnecessary. In the words of Frankl, "the egotist can only benefit from considering others, and conversely, the altruist—for the very sake of the others—must always take care of himself."[37]

Whether, subjectively speaking, an individual derives ego satisfaction from altruistic conduct is ultimately irrelevant. Such conduct is objectively desirable because continuous unfettered clashes of selfish egos with each other would create a forbidding climate of living. The perpetual friction engendered

---

35. R. RINGER, LOOKING OUT FOR #1 50 (1977).
36. *Ibid.*
37. FRANKL, *supra* note 24, at 68.

by the remorseless struggle for personal advantage would tend to lead to the disintegration and ultimate destruction of society. Unconcern for the feelings and interests of others is a result which sane human beings cannot wish for.

This does not mean that conflicts between egotistic and altruistic motivations should always be decided in favor of the latter. An individual engaged in a difficult and time-consuming assignment may sometimes have to give priority to it over obligations to family members and friends. A creative thinker may have to shun or reduce personal communication with the public, although many people would benefit from it. Since responsibility involves duties both to the individual himself and to others, difficult decisions may have to be made in borderline situations whether the existential responsibility for self-actualization should or should not take precedence over the obligations owed to other human beings.

Finally, a suggestion might be made concerning the proper attitude of parents and educators toward the development of egotistic and altruistic inclinations in the young person. There can be little doubt that, in the life of an individual, an egotistic period precedes the advent of socialization. An infant in his early years is, in the words of Allport, "an unsocialized horror."[38] If nothing is done by parents and educators to inculcate other-regarding attitudes in the young person, the unsocialized state is likely to persist into adulthood, with the result that such a person will be resented and shunned by his environment.[39] Generally speaking, the development of the unselfish side of an individual's personality requires encouragement and support from the outside, while self-seeking is instinctive and self-originating. This last statement is subject to the qualification that the higher manifestations of ego-assertion, which are epitomized in the notion of self-perfection, may be in need of stimulation from the environment; as was pointed out earlier in this chapter, the inertial and homeostatic tendencies in man's nature may easily get the better of his upward drive.

---

38. ALLPORT, *supra* note 7, at 28.
39. Additional reasons for strengthening the social side of man's nature are set forth *supra* Chapter 1 (C).

CHAPTER 5

Responsibility in Sexual and Family Relationships

A. RESPONSIBILITY TOWARD SEXUAL PARTNERS

The smallest community, which nature itself has brought about by dividing mankind into two sexes, is the union of the male with the female. Relations between a man and a woman may be of a fleeting, temporary, or permanent nature. Where relations of the first kind are mercenary in character and not prohibited by law, no serious problems of responsibility will normally arise, except perhaps the duty to warn a partner of a health hazard. Where fleeting relations are of a nonmercenary character, the possibility exists that one partner, especially the female one, is used by the other as a mere means for the satisfaction of a biological drive. When both parties are, explicitly or implicitly, in agreement that no continuing obligations should follow the casual sexual contact, no debatable issue is presented, assuming that the legal order is disinterested in the situation.[1] On the other hand, if consent to enter into intimacy was on one side based on deep attachment and in the expectation of a continuing relationship (an expectation which may have been deliberately aroused by the

---

1. Some states of the Union still have laws penalizing fornication.

other side), a moral problem does arise.[2] Since the obligation not to injure others extends—at least morally—to the emotional and affective sphere of the human personality, an awareness of the problem may furnish a cogent reason for not commencing the relationship or, if it has already been entered into, to continue it in some manner which will alleviate the mental suffering of the other person.

When a relationship between persons of different sex is of a more lasting character, its termination by one side against the wishes of the other may produce a somewhat similar predicament. A responsible person will not simply yield to the impulse of the moment but conscientiously weigh the effect which a decision to put an end to the relation will have on the companion. The principle of responsibility calls for a solution which will minimize the hurt inflicted on the partner to the greatest degree possible under the circumstances.

A short story by John Galsworthy entitled "The Apple Tree" presents a problem in this area of human relations in an artistically brilliant manner.[3] A young Englishman named Frank Ashurst went on an extended hiking trip with a friend. His knee gave out, and it became necessary for him to seek shelter at a farmhouse to rest his leg for a few days, while his friend was returning home. On the farm he met a seventeen-year-old girl named Megan, a niece of the owner. She was a country girl from Wales, a true creature of nature, like a flower growing in the hills, simple, unsophisticated, beautiful and pure. Frank, on the other hand, was a product of the upper English middle class, brought up in London, highly educated, reflective, sensitive, and cultured. He became greatly attracted to the girl, and she fell in love with him deeply and intensely.

One night they met under an apple tree near the farmhouse. She told him of her love and said "I shall die if I can't be with you." He told her that on the next day he would go to the next town to buy her some clothes, and they would then steal away and travel to London. He added that, if she loved him well enough, they would perhaps get married some day, whereupon she replied: "Oh no! I could not, I only want to be with you."

---

2. Perhaps also a legal problem, as indicated by Marvin v. Marvin, *infra* note 8.

3. J. GALSWORTHY, FIVE TALES 187-257 (1918).

The next day Frank went to a nearby town to purchase a dress for Megan. He could not make up his mind what to buy, because it now seemed incredible to him that Megan could ever be dressed save in the rough tweed skirt and coarse blouse she was wearing. Walking through the town, he met an old friend who invited him to lunch with his three young sisters. The girls urged Frank to go to the beach with them in the afternoon and, after some initial hesitation, he accepted. He overstayed his time, so that it became impossible for him to return to the farm that night. He sent a telegram to Megan's aunt, advising her that he would return the following morning. Instead, he stayed with his friend and the three girls several more days, becoming quite interested in one of the sisters, Stella. She was an educated girl of his own class, with similar manners, and able to share his ideas about the world. His feelings for Megan had not diminished, but he knew now that he could never marry her. He felt extremely guilty for not returning to the farm to carry out the plan on which he had agreed with Megan. But the thought of making her his mistress and then discarding her, perhaps after a few weeks of passionate love, was also intolerable to him. He was certain that such a course of action would destroy her. After seriously struggling with this dilemma, he finally decided to abandon Megan.

One year later he married Stella. On their silver-wedding anniversary, they drove to the town where they had first met. On the way they stopped for lunch at a place which he recognized as being near the farm where he had stayed twenty-six years ago. There was an unmarked grave at the place. When Stella went off to do some painting, Frank walked to the farm and questioned an old laborer about the grave. He was told that it was the burial place of a girl who had drowned herself in the stream flowing by the apple tree, because a young man she was in love with had, contrary to his promise, not returned to her. Frank asked himself what he had done wrong, but he could not find an answer.

Sigmund Freud was greatly impressed with this story. In his one-sentence interpretation he said that the story "brings home to us how the life of present-day civilized people leaves no room for the simple natural love of two human beings."[4] The context

---

4. S. FREUD, CIVILIZATION AND ITS DISCONTENTS 52, footnote 2 (J. Strachey transl. 1961).

in which this remark is made discloses a critical attitude on the part of Freud toward Frank Ashurst's failure to consummate his budding love affair with Megan. Since Frank's refusal to elope with the girl, as he had promised, caused her to take her own life, it is indeed perfectly justified to raise the question whether even a brief period of passionate fulfillment would not have been a preferable solution for both. Did Frank take an oversensitive, exaggerated view of his responsibility toward the girl when he decided to desert her, being convinced that a mere temporary love affair would, in view of her character and her intense affection for him, destroy her in the end?

Simone de Beauvoir, a woman who cannot be said to have old-fashioned opinions regarding the relations between the sexes, has stated that "the peculiar nature of her eroticism and the difficulties that beset a life of freedom urge woman toward monogamy."[5] Even though this statement may be an overgeneralization, it may be true that many women seek attachment for life to one man. If Frank was certain that Megan belonged to this class of women, he might have inflicted irreparable harm on her by going through with their original plan to be together, knowing that he would not stay with her for a long time. As things turned out, he wounded the girl mortally by taking his responsibilities very seriously. He could not have predicted her suicide, but he realized that he would grievously hurt her by his decision to abandon her.

Max Stirner would have argued that human beings should make the most out of their lives and enjoy themselves to the maximum degree, regardless of the feelings and fates of others.[6] Albert Schweitzer, on the other hand, thought that a person had a primary moral responsibility not to harm others by his actions.[7] It is debatable whether or not Frank made the right decision under the circumstances; but a flat denial that he was confronted with a genuine moral problem would be incompatible with a humanistic and civilized attitude toward human affairs.

In recent years, the law has paid some attention to

---

5. S. DE BEAUVOIR, THE SECOND SEX 694 (H. Parshley transl. 1968).
6. See *supra* Chapter 1 (C), text preceding note 8.
7. A. SCHWEITZER, CIVILIZATION AND ETHICS 259-260 (C. Campion transl. 1946).

relationships between the sexes which formerly were thought to involve only moral problems. In the case of *Marvin v. Marvin*,[8] a woman who had lived with the defendant for approximately six years claimed a portion of his property as compensation for her services as companion, housekeeper, and hostess. The Supreme Court of California held that her request should be granted if she could prove an express or implied contract with the defendant for a sharing of his earnings and property acquired during the time of their relationship. At the subsequent trial conducted to establish the existence or nonexistence of such a contract, the defendant testified "that he wanted a relationship of no responsibility, and that the defendant agreed thereto."[9] The Court concluded that no express or implied agreement for the sharing of earnings and property had been proved by the plaintiff, but it awarded her a sum of money on grounds of fairness and equity.

The case raises the question, among others, whether the law should sanction an agreement between two parties entering into an intimate relationship that one of them, or both, would assume no responsibility of any kind toward the other. It would seem that no objection should be raised against such a compact if made by mature persons who are aware of the likely consequences of such an understanding. If these conditions are not met, it would seem that the partners assume certain responsibilities regarding their mutual well-being which last beyond the duration of their companionship. The reasons supporting this position have been adverted to earlier. The human, and particularly the emotional impact of such a relationship is normally so strong that each person has entered into the life and personality of the other in a significant way, and a subsequent separation will in many cases not wipe out this deep mutual involvement. The extent to which the law should take cognizance of the moral ties thus created cannot be answered by any generally valid formula; the court in the *Marvin* case based the right to a monetary recovery on the peculiar combination of circumstances present in that case.

---

8. 18 Cal.3d 660, 134 Cal. Rptr. 815, 557 P.2d 106 (1976).

9. Marvin v. Marvin, Superior Court of Los Angeles County, 5 FAM. L. RPTR. 3077, at 3078 (1979).

B. RESPONSIBILITY TOWARD SPOUSES

When two persons enter into a marital status, the traditional ethics of most societies have assumed at least an original intent to form a permanent union. The Roman Catholic Church has gone further than other religions in giving effect to an assumption of permanency; it has prohibited divorce, except by special dispensation from the highest authority of the Church. Most religions and secular orders have permitted divorce (sometimes on an unequal basis for men and women), but have often regarded it as an *ultima ratio* to be resorted to only for very strong reasons. Today, termination of marriage has become easy and widespread in most countries of the Western world. Although the law may allow divorce only in case of an irretrievable breakdown of marriage, little effort is expended by the courts in requiring proof of such breakdown. In California and some other states of the United States, the desire of one spouse to dissolve the marital bond is for all practical purposes sufficient to end a marriage. Indeed, there is little doubt that a divorce is sometimes obtained for slight or trivial reasons.

Even in states permitting easy divorce, the entering of a divorce decree does not necessarily mean that the relations between the former spouses become totally severed. The legal obligation to support the economically weaker partner often survives the dissolution of the marriage because the courts in most states of the United States, and in other countries, have power to award alimony to either the wife or the husband, if they consider such an award fair and equitable.[10]

The notion that support obligations may continue after termination of the marital status has been criticized in some quarters,[11] but it appears to persist on the strength of the traditional belief that marriage is a partnership intended for life, and that the responsibilities originating from this original

---

10. On the right to alimony see H. KRAUSE, FAMILY LAW IN A NUTSHELL 329-345 (1977). The United States Supreme Court has held that a statutory scheme of imposing alimony obligations on husbands but not wives violates the Equal Protection Clause of the Federal Constitution. Orr v. Orr, 99 S. Ct. 1102 (1979).

11. See KRAUSE, *supra* note 10, at 332, 365.

intent cannot be entirely erased by subsequent events. When children have issued from the marital union, arrangements for child support and custody will often require some degree of cooperation between the parents in the interest of the children, so that here again the bond created by the parents by virtue of their marriage is not cut off by the dissolution of the marriage.

It is widely agreed today by psychiatrists, social workers, and others that the effect of divorce upon children of the marriage, especially young ones, is normally traumatic and may leave permanent scars.[12] Some authorities have argued that a continuation of a marriage characterized by a constant display of open enmity is more damaging to the offspring than its dissolution. Whether or not this is true depends on the degree of unconcealed friction existing between the spouses, and the extent to which such friction has an injurious effect on the children.

Frequently divorce is not prompted by a deep-seated aversion to the other spouse or serious mutual incompatibility, but by a desire to share one's life with another person. If separation in such a case is resisted or strongly resented by the other spouse, it is clear that the step is essentially a self-regarding one, often motivated by a desire for a variety of partners and new experiences. These cannot be regarded as sufficient reasons for an act which may cause irreparable mental suffering to the rejected spouse and, if there are children, is likely to have a deleterious effect upon them.[13] Since the damaging or the psychic destruction, for hedonistic motives, of a person with whom one may have shared many years of common experiences is also apt to saddle the deserting spouse with strong feelings of guilt, this effect may outbalance the newly-won happiness.

In addition, a certain amount of stability in the home and trust between marital partners appears to be necessary to enable each of them to function well in society and vocational life. Only very strong personalities can combine flexible sexual

---

12. See, e.g., Wallerstein & Kelly, *The Effects of Parental Divorce: Experiences of the Preschool Child*, 14 J. CHILD PSYCH. 600 (1975); Wallerstein & Kelly, *The Effects of Parental Divorce: The Adolescent Experience*, in 3 THE CHILD IN HIS FAMILY 479 (E. Anthony & C. Koupernik ed. 1974).
13. See in this connection B. Bodenheimer, *Reflections on the Grounds for Divorce*, 8 J. FAM. L. 179, 190-193 (1968).

relations or a permanent "open season" with a productive life and work accomplishments. A persistent fear of a termination of the relationship on the part of one spouse will in many cases produce psychological effects detrimental to vocational performance. For this and other reasons, there is merit in the suggestion of existentialist scholar Hazel Barnes that "in society as it is presently set up, a mutual commitment to the love which forsakes all others is probably the most rewarding for most people."[14] The only *absolute* demand, in her opinion, is honesty and mutual agreement on the part of both persons as to what their commitments to each other really are and what each wants them to be.[15] It seems clear that these commitments, to be meaningful, must include reciprocal respect and concern for the partner's well-being.

These observations do not mean to suggest that divorce motivated by a unilateral desire for a new marriage is hardly ever justified. However, there must be clear indications (1) that in spite of every bona fide effort to save the marriage, its continuation would lead to certain frustration and mutual disappointment, and (2) that entering into a new union is well-nigh indispensable to one partner's further growth and effective functioning in society. The necessity for thoroughly weighing these considerations in one's mind stems from the fact that making another person part of one's life entails not only privileges but also obligations. These obligations are partly rooted in human nature itself, which includes in its characteristic traits an expectation of concern and respect by others for one's feelings and interests. This trait, in turn, evokes the application of the Golden Rule. The marital partner confronted with a crucial choice such as described above must ask himself what his own reaction would be in case of a reversal of roles.[16]

C. RESPONSIBILITY TOWARD CHILDREN

The problem of responsibility of parents toward their children has in recent decades assumed special significance because of the widespread existence of child neglect and

---

14. H. BARNES, AN EXISTENTIALIST ETHICS 359 (1967).
15. *Ibid.*
16. See *supra* Chapter 1 (C) and *infra* Chapter 6 (A).

juvenile delinquency. Large numbers of juvenile offenders come from homes which have been disrupted by divorce or separation. Another substantial percentage of such offenders come from households in which the children are alienated from their parents. It is widely conceded that children from disrupted or disturbed homes are much more likely to be exposed to crime-producing influences than children who are attached to their parents and receive loving care.[17]

It has also been found that weakened or severed bonds between parents and children are apt to cause behavioral changes in the children. Among these are irritability, sleep problems, depression, heightened aggressiveness, anxiety about future marriage, and cognitive confusion.[18] An unstable home environment is not conducive to psychological health and social adaptation of young persons.[19]

Under these circumstances, indifference or hostility displayed by parents toward their children must be regarded as a violation of responsibility. Openly manifested and persistent friction between the parents is also likely to have an adverse effect upon the children. The problem becomes aggravated when divorce or separation occurs; the impact of such events upon children is often traumatic, at least for a time. There is little doubt that an intact family life sustained by mutual affection tends to protect a child from antisocial influences of peer groups and neighborhoods; a well-integrated home in which a great deal of time is spent with the children lessens the attractions of delinquent gangs.[20]

17. T. HIRSCHI, CAUSES OF DELINQUENCY 85-88, 99 (1969); S.&E. GLUECK, UNRAVELING JUVENILE DELINQUENCY 121-125, 133 (1950); Monahan, *Family Status and the Delinquent Child,* 35 SOCIAL FORCES 250, 251-253, 258 (1957); F. NYE, FAMILY RELATIONSHIPS AND DELINQUENT BEHAVIOR 71-75 (1958); E. ELDEFONSO, LAW ENFORCEMENT AND THE YOUTHFUL OFFENDER 81-82, 168 (2d ed. 1973).

18. Wallerstein & Kelly, *The Effects of Parental Divorce: Experiences of the Preschool Child, supra* note 12, at 602; Wallerstein & Kelly, *The Effects of Parental Divorce: The Adolescent Experience, supra* note 12, at 485-486, 499-500.

19. W. GLASSER, THE IDENTITY SOCIETY 133 (1972); GLUECK, *supra* note 17, at 125; J. GOLDSTEIN, A. FREUD, & A. SOLNIT, BEYOND THE BEST INTERESTS OF THE CHILD 18, 32 (1973).

20. HIRSCHI, *supra* note 17, at 85.

It must, of course, be realized that the conditions of modern life are not necessarily conducive to the maintenance of a wholesome home atmosphere. When both parents work, they are often tired during their free hours and seek relaxation and diversion; communication with the children is likely to suffer under these circumstances. It is also true that today men and women often tend to give priority to their own desires and goals as individuals. Children in that situation take second place.[21] In the words of William Goode,

> people pay lip service to family stability. But for themselves, they want something else, a bit more. They want more personal freedom, more self-seeking, more room for developing their own interests and personalities, and less responsibility toward others. Most of us are not willing to accept the deep, real restrictions on choices that a strengthened family life would require.... [I]f we move toward a moral regeneration, if we change the major directions in which our society moves, we shall do so only by accepting the greater restrictions on personal choices and heavier demands for personal sacrifice that stable family life requires.[22]

Under present conditions, the establishment of adequate daycare centers for preschool children would alleviate some of the problems which parental inattention and neglect are bound to cause;[23] but, generally speaking, the responsibility of parents to show love and concern for their offspring is one that cannot be delegated to third persons. That the existence of alienation between parents and children is widespread is, among other indications, demonstrated by the fact that there are close to 500,000 teenage alcoholics in this country, and that suicide is the second leading cause of death for people between the ages of fifteen and twenty-four.[24]

---

21. B. Bodenheimer, *Foreword*, 6 U.C.D.L. REV. viii (1973).
22. Goode, *State Intervention and the Family: Problems of Policy*, 1976 BRIGH. YOUNG U.L. REV. 715, 720-721.
23. Bronfenbrenner, *The Origins of Alienation*, 53 SCIENTIFIC AMERICAN 231, 234-235 (1974).
24. S. GORDON, LONELY IN AMERICA 50 (1976).

Ch. 5 Responsibility in Sexual and Family Relationships

Another problem involving parental responsibility is the maintenance of a proper balance between pedagogical guidance and laissez-faire. During the earliest stages of a child's life, the exercise of authority must necessarily take precedence over permissiveness. The parents will have to decide how to feed the child, how to keep it clean, and when to put it to sleep at night. They will also have to determine what kinds of play and other activities are suitable for infants at successive stages in their development.

Today it is generally agreed, however, that the ability to use one's own judgment and make one's own decisions should be fostered in children as early as possible; unlimited dependence on parents is likely to hamper the growth of young persons. Responsible parents will realize, on the other hand, that adolescents in many respects lack the experience for making well-considered judgments, and that they need direction in a number of areas relating to the conduct of life. Among these areas are nutrition, relations between the sexes, and the basic norms for social intercourse with fellow human beings.

Since the proper kind of nutrition is an indispensable factor in the growth of a young person, some exercise of supervisory control by parents is necessary. Although a strange "right to be unhealthy" has been advocated by one scholar,[25] it is not likely that this writer would wish to extend this "right" to persons in the stage of early development.

Naturally, the relations between the sexes present special hazards to very young persons. Few people would deny this fact. However, a radical protagonist of childrens' rights, Richard Farson, has advocated "freedom for children to conduct their own sexual lives with no more restrictions than adults."[26] This writer also proposed that all sexual activity (apparently including incest) be decriminalized,[27] and that children be permitted to read any obscene book and see any pornographic film.[28]

A policy of extreme permissiveness with respect to sex is

---

25. Shuman, *The Right to be Unhealthy*, 22 WAYNE L. REV. 61 (1975). For a discussion of Shuman's views see *supra* Chapter 4 (C).
26. R. FARSON, BIRTHRIGHTS 152-153 (1974).
27. *Id.* at 148-151, 153.
28. *Id.* at 135.

certainly not a satisfactory approach to the upbringing of children. The strong emotional impact which sexual activity has upon individuals presents special psychological hazards to the young. To the dangers which confront them must be added teenage pregnancy and contraction of venereal disease. Intimate relations between men and women require a certain degree of maturity which children have not yet reached. Furthermore, urgent educational tasks may suffer a setback if sex activity—as is likely to happen under a policy of unlimited laissez-faire—becomes an absorbing interest at an early age.[29]

This does not mean that exposure of children to the sexual area should be tabooed, as was customary in the not so remote past. A frank discussion of facts and problems in this area at an appropriate age should be a responsibility of the parents, along with the schools, because ignorance or misinformation may have fateful consequences for young persons.

An equally serious question relates to the need for moral education in a broader sense, involving the observance of a general code of social conduct. Today, many persons hold a belief in a situational ethic which makes the formulation of moral directives largely a matter of individual judgment.[30] If this position is taken, an inculcation of general ethical standards as part of the educational process would be futile and inappropriate. However, as will be shown in Chapter 6, certain fundamental ethical rules governing human relations do exist in all societies and are widely observed, notwithstanding a relaxation of some specific moral standards in recent decades. It is therefore a command of practical reason to acquaint the young generation with these rules. Moreover, the most basic norms of ethical behavior have become incorporated into the law. Ignorance of the law is no excuse from liability under the law of crimes and torts. This makes it mandatory for parents and other educators to insist on compliance with those general standards of conduct which are not matters of individual choice.

It is by no means easy to combine the fostering of independence and self-reliance in young persons with a

---
29. See in this connection also *infra* Chapter 8 (D).
30. Situation ethics is discussed *infra* Chapter 6 (C).

reasonable measure of disciplinary control. It requires much less display of discriminating judgment if we are either in the habit of giving strict orders or refrain altogether from providing guidance to our children. Both extremes fail to prepare the young for the demands of responsible adulthood. Both extremes fail to meet the requirements of parental responsibility. Autocratic parenthood stifles initiative, while a complete laissez-faire attitude breeds overly demanding, selfish, and dissatisfied individuals.[31] Furthermore, in every society the majority of people are required to carry out imposed tasks in their daily work, while at other times they are expected to use their own judgment intelligently. Thus individuals, in order to become competent participants in the social process, must be prepared for self-direction as well as for direction by others.[32] We are confronted here with a complex problem of education which cannot be solved by a set of simple formulae.

What are the consequences of a disregard of parental responsibility? The area in which parents enjoy autonomy in the treatment and education of their children is quite extensive. However, minimum standards for the exercise of responsibility by parents are set by law. For example, there are statutes requiring school attendance and prohibiting child labor. Obvious instances of child neglect, such as failure to provide food, clothing, and urgent medical care, and severe cases of child abuse, such as abandonment and physical cruelty, are held to justify interference by the state. The relevant statutory provisions are usually formulated in flexible language and leave a great deal of discretion to the courts. The most common sanctions are surveillance of parents' conduct within the home by social agencies with or without education or counseling services, temporary removal of the child to foster parents who

---

31. See A. ADLER, SOCIAL INTEREST 45-48 (J. Linton & R. Vaughan transl. 1964).
32. See in this connection A. WHITEHEAD, THE AIMS OF EDUCATION, Ch. 3 (1929). Cf. the following statement by the psychiatrist H. EYSENCK, CRIME AND PERSONALITY 172 (1977): "Clearly, the path to follow is through a middle ground, to treat children with a sufficient degree of severity to achieve the conditioning required by society, but not to treat them so severely that they fall prey to neurotic disorders."

may be relatives, and, as a measure of last resort, permanent termination of parental rights.[33]

The proper scope of parental autonomy is at the present time a subject of dispute in the United States. Some authors have taken the position that the right of the state to intervene in the affairs of the family should be kept at a minimum.[34] It has been argued, for example, that the government's obligation to protect children from inadequate performance by their parents should be restricted to instances of infliction of severe physical or emotional injury, sexual abuse, and unwillingness to provide sustenance or acutely necessary medical treatment.[35] It has also been proposed that judicial discretion to intervene in a family should be severely limited by defining in advance and with some precision those harms which justify governmental action.[36]

Such proposals raise serious questions. The rights of children to proper care and freedom from abuse are not necessarily infringed by single, definable acts of parents resulting in immediate and palpable damage to the child. These rights may be violated by forms of neglect which are relatively minor when viewed in isolation, but which will wreak havoc with the child's physical and mental health when continued over a prolonged period of time. Furthermore, there might be combinations of various misfeasances, such as indifference to educational or medical needs, ostentatious denial of affection, and other instances of maltreatment which in their aggregate justify an intervention by the authorities,

33. KRAUSE, *supra* note 10, at 232-244; S. KATZ, WHEN PARENTS FAIL 1-89 (1971).

34. See, e.g., Wald, *State Intervention on Behalf of 'Neglected' Children: A Search for Realistic Standards*, 27 STAN. L. REV. 985, 986-987 (1975); Levy, *The Rights of Parents*, 1976 BRIGH. YOUNG U.L. REV. 693; Goldstein, *Medical Care for the Child at Risk*, 86 YALE L.J. 645, 667 (1977).

35. Wald, *supra* note 34, at 1008.

36. Wald, *State Invervention on Behalf of Neglected Children: Standards for Removal of Children from Their Homes, Monitoring the Status of Children in Foster Care, and Termination of Parental Rights*, 28 STAN. L. REV. 623, 639-640 (1976); Mnookin, *Child Custody Adjudication: Judicial Functions in the Face of Indeterminacy*, 39 LAW & CONTEMP. PROB. (No. 3) 226, 268-272, 277-279 (1975).

although each single act or omission might not be sufficient to warrant it. These situations cannot be captured in precise legal definitions of parental derelictions of duty, and some measure of judicial discretion is inevitable to cope with the problem effectively.

A judge of the Family Court in New York City, Nanette Dembitz, has proposed a new scheme of preventive reporting to guard against the danger of a step-by-step undermining of a child's well-being due to sustained parental inability to give proper care.[37] State laws already require that doctors, school teachers, and other professionals working with children report suspected acts of parental abuse to a child protection agency. Judge Dembitz maintains that, among others, "children whose parents ignore their serious ailments and injuries . . . are never seen by those who might report them" (under the mandates of these laws).[38] She would require reporting, in certain specified situations such as chronic mental or physical illness of parents, narcotics or alcohol addiction, or teenage parenthood, situations which are apt to lead to incapacity of parenting. "If neither a parent nor relative can give a child minimal care, even with assistance from social services," Judge Dembitz says, the child should be placed with stable "affection-extending" foster or adoptive parents. But, she warns, placement must be early, "before children have lived so long in turmoil that they are inaccessible to love and guidance."[39]

The obstacle to requiring such reporting is concern for the parents' privacy. This, of course, is a legitimate concern, but it must be balanced against the public interest in the protection of children. We cannot close our eyes to the fact that considerable disintegration of family life has taken place in the United States and other countries, and that the statistical figures for child neglect are alarmingly high.[40] Public intervention in cases where persistent parental indifference to the needs of a child (whatever the cause) may in the course of time destroy or

---

37. Dembitz, *Preventing Youth Crime by Preventing Child Neglect*, 65 A.B.A.J. 920 (1979).

38. *Id.* at 922.

39. *Id.* at 923.

40. See, among many others, Margaret Mead in Redbook, February 1977, at 91-92, 154-156; Bronfenbrenner, *supra* note 23, at 231-234.

weaken his health and character must be faced as an unavoidable means of saving children for productive lives. Let us remember that a young generation which is physically and mentally fit for life in society is our major insurance for a promising future.

D. RESPONSIBILITY TOWARD PARENTS

The responsibility which children owe their parents is expressed in terse language in the Fifth Commandment of the Decalogue: "Honor thy father and thy mother."[41] Traditional civilization in China and Japan has given special weight to this duty in the doctrine of filial piety. Children were strongly imbued with the obligation to be loyal and respectful to their parents, and they had to render near-absolute obedience to the head of the family. The overriding importance of these duties was emphasized in the teachings of Confucius, who expressed his conviction that "civilization commenced with filial piety."[42] Those who were known for their filial devotion were accorded high social esteem, a fact which was often of distinct benefit to them in their later life.[43]

While in China the duties of children toward their parents were defined by morality and custom rather than by law, in Rome the authority of the family father over his children was firmly recognized by the law. This authority was originally unlimited. It extended not only over the sons and daughters (except daughters who had become emancipated by marriage), but also over the children of sons and the sons' remote descendants, regardless of whether or not these persons lived in the parental home.[44] According to the Roman law, all of these descendants owed a duty of absolute obedience to the *pater familias*. The only surveillance that was exercised over abuses of paternal power in the earlier period of Roman history was through the prerogative of moral censure entrusted to public

---

41. Exodus 20:12.
42. T. CHENG, CHINA MOULDED BY CONFUCIUS 166 (1947).
43. *Id.* at 170.
44. On parental authority in Rome see H. JOLOWICZ, HISTORICAL INTRODUCTION TO THE STUDY OF ROMAN LAW 118-119, 248-249 (2d ed. 1965); M. KASER, DAS RÖMISCHE PRIVATRECHT: ERSTER ABSCHNITT 341-345 (2d ed. 1971).

Ch. 5 Responsibility in Sexual and Family Relationships

officials known as censors.[45] In the later periods of Roman history, beginning with the period of the Principate, the powers of the family father were gradually restricted.[46] During the Middle Ages and the early centuries of the modern era, parental authority remained strong, although it never attained the dimensions of the Roman *patria potestas*. Fathers were free to make all decisions relating to the welfare of their minor children, as long as they remained within the limits of the law. The child's duty of obedience remained a mainstay of the social and legal order. In recent times, legislatures and courts have abandoned the father's primary authority and given equal powers to both parents.

The weakening of family bonds in modern Western society has placed in doubt the extent of the children's responsibility to obey their parents and respect their wishes. Some writers discuss the rights of children without reference to their obligations. In the past, it was generally assumed that it was the child's responsibility to accept the decision of his parents in regard to the choice of school. In recent times, some authors have suggested that each child should be entirely free to decide whether or not to go to school (including pre-school) or to get his education in some other way.[47] In the words of John Holt,

> Young people should have the right to control and direct their own learning, that is, to decide what they want to learn, and when, where, how, how much, how fast, and with what help they want to learn it. To be still more specific, I want them to have the right to decide if, when, how much, and by whom they want to be *taught* and the right to decide whether they want to learn in a school and if so which one and for how much of the time.[48]

Such proposals would, of course, not only put an end to the parents' right to make educational decisions for young children

---

45. On the powers of the censors see *supra* Chapter 1 (A).
46. For a more extensive survey of this development see E. BODENHEIMER, POWER, LAW, AND SOCIETY 154-156 (1973).
47. J. HOLT, ESCAPE FROM CHILDHOOD 240-248 (1974); R. FARSON, BIRTHRIGHTS 96-97, 106-112 (1974).
48. HOLT, *supra* note 47, at 240.

which are binding on them; these proposals would also require repeal of all compulsory education laws. One author has made the further suggestion that children should have farreaching rights to decide whether they wish to live at home or prefer to live in another family, or in a commune or institution (regardless of whether the child is well or ill treated).[49] Such proposals are highly vulnerable to criticism. It is indisputable that children should have certain rights; the most important among them are the right to proper care and education, and the right to be decently treated. On the other hand, children lack certain capabilities and experiences possessed by normal adults which handicap them in making well-considered judgments in various areas of life. In these areas, the child should be required to accept the decisions of his parents. This responsibility should not, however, be regarded as an absolute one. It should be held that a child, after reaching a certain age, may refuse to comply with parental decisions which are oppressive, palpably unreasonable in light of prevailing standards, or incompatible with his dignity as a human being. If necessary, a child, with the help of a competent representative, should be able to invoke the aid of a court in fighting against an unconscionable act of his parents.

The responsibility owed by children to their parents after the latter have reached old age raises other difficult questions. In the period of agricultural civilization, there was always room for the old people on the farm run by one or several of their children. There was available a wing in the farmhouse to shelter them, and there was ordinarily some household work that kept them occupied. These conditions made old people an economic asset to the younger generation and at the same time helped preserve their own morale and self-respect.

Today most families no longer live in homes in which one can build on a room or wing to house aging parents. The income of old people has in many countries been reduced to a modest pension, perhaps supplemented by social security. They are often forced to lower their standard of living substantially, feeling at the same time useless, lonely, and

---

49. FARSON, *supra* note 47, at 43, 58-61. See also the remarks of Professor Robert Green in RIGHTS OF CHILDREN: REPORT OF THE FIRST INTERNATIONAL CONFERENCE ON CHILDREN'S RIGHTS 9 (1972).

unwanted. Conditions in old-age homes are frequently appalingly bad.[50]

In the Western world, there has also occurred an erosion of the high respect that has been paid to the aged in other civilizations. Many grown-up children today devote little attention to their parents. This is not necessarily due to ill will or neglect, but may be caused by distances in large cities or different domiciles. In society at large, there is also a tendency to ignore the old, since they are no longer a productive asset to the community.

These conditions should certainly be alleviated to the maximum extent possible, and the responsibility of the children toward their parents must necessarily play a major part in any improvement. This responsibility is not based on gratitude of the children to the parents for having brought them into the world; the act of procreation is not intended as a favor to the child. The responsibility stems from the general duty of concern and respect for other human beings, which obviously is enhanced considerably by family bonds. It is also supported by the Golden Rule: those who in the prime of their lives do not respect the older generation cannot expect to receive much consideration when they themselves become old and infirm.

---

50. For a thorough discussion of the problems of living to which old people are exposed see S. DE BEAUVOIR, OLD AGE 216-277 (P. O'Brian transl. 1972).

CHAPTER 6

Responsibility Toward Fellow Human Beings

A. PRELIMINARY OBSERVATIONS

The ambit of responsibility in its social aspects is not limited to intimate personal unions and family relationships. It encompasses the whole field of neighborly, vocational, and even some casual relations between human beings. The question is how this position can be justified. Are not the tasks of life hard and exacting enough to make it sufficient that, except for certain special situations, we should be held responsible only for our own well-being and self-realization? What psychological and ethical considerations could possibly lead us to the conclusion that in some respects we should become our brothers' and our sisters' keepers?

A partial answer to this question was offered in the first chapter of this book.[1] To the considerations there put forward must be added the obvious truth that no human being is a self-sufficient entity. Every person is linked to a number of other persons by a variety of reciprocal bonds. These bonds originate in the necessity of conducting multifarious joint activities, such as producing material goods, educating the young, caring for the sick, carrying on the functions of government. Someone might argue that in a collaborative enterprise everybody should

---

1. See *supra* Chapter 1 (C). It was pointed out there that, under the teaching of the Golden Rule, we cannot expect others to act responsibly and considerately towards us unless we do so ourselves.

do his or her share without regard to what others are doing. In reality, some degree of group-consciousness on the part of the members of an organization is necessary to build and maintain morale and cohesion. New employees expect some help and advice from experienced co-workers or colleagues. All expect appreciation of their contribution and advancement of their status if deserved. They also desire some courtesy in human relations and consideration of their reasonable claims.

The obligation to show concern and respect for others is not limited to organizational activities. It extends to the whole area of human relations.[2] A wholly self-regarding individual, devoid of any sense of obligation toward his fellow human beings, will usually encounter so little consideration and sympathetic response from society that his aim of self-realization will be defeated rather than furthered by his antisocial or asocial attitude. Stirner was well aware that his philosophy of untrammeled self-seeking would lead to a war of everybody against everybody, a consequence which he was willing to accept.[3] But the famous English thinker who declared that universal warfare was the condition of mankind in a natural, unorganized state also pointed out that there is implanted in human beings a desire for peace and harmony. He knew that there exists an urge for creating a livable world in which there is room for constructive achievement, although conflict and strife cannot be altogether banished from human life.[4] The principle of responsibility in its other-regarding aspects is grounded upon the insight that without an endeavor on the part of all or most to exhibit concern and respect for their fellow human beings, this world would be a highly inhospitable and even repulsive place to live in.

---

2. Ronald Dworkin has said: "Government must treat those whom it governs with concern, that is, as human beings who are capable of suffering and frustration, and with respect, that is, as human beings who are capable of forming and acting on intelligent conceptions of how their lives should be lived." R. DWORKIN, TAKING RIGHTS SERIOUSLY 272 (1977). It may be assumed that Dworkin would not wish to limit the right to concern and respect to action by the government.
3. M. STIRNER, THE EGO AND HIS OWN 257, 260 (S. Byington transl. 1963). See the discussion of Stirner's views *supra* Chapter 1 (C).
4. T. HOBBES, DE CIVE, Ch. I. 3-7; Ch. II. 2 (S. Lamprecht ed. 1949).

Jean-Paul Sartre has said that a human being is responsible not only for himself but for everyone else.[5] Although this statement appears exaggerated in its sweeping breadth, it possesses a healthy core. Whatever action is taken or whatever attitude is expressed by me may have an impact on others, and these others may in turn influence additional persons by what they do or say. If my philosophy of life is communicated publicly by word or print, its imitative reach may be even greater; and in the case of a person endowed with charisma, the snowballing effect of his message may be overwhelming. When everybody cares deeply about that which he can influence by his actions, the world becomes a better place to live in.

B. PRINCIPLED AND INDIVIDUALIZED MORALITY

The further question arises whether responsible conduct toward one's fellow human beings should be exercised in the form of definite moral principles adopted as a strict guide for one's action, or whether the display of responsibility ought to take place in a non-normative, individualized fashion in response to the exigencies of a concrete situation. The first alternative is epitomized by the Decalogue in the Old Testament, which contains ten pithily and apodictively formulated commandments.[6] The second alternative is illustrated by Jean-Paul Sartre's assertion that outside ourselves "we find no values or commands to turn to which legitimize our conduct."[7]

The first alternative carries with it the drawback of overrigidity, the second one that of overflexibility. A code of norms is usually not workable if it is interpreted and applied with undeviating faithfulness to the letter of the text. Although the Ten Commandments retain their general validity today, it needs to be recognized that some of them are subject to narrowly-circumscribed exceptions. The command "Thou shalt not kill" does not apply to homicide in self-defense, to the

---

5. J. SARTRE, EXISTENTIALISM 21 (B. Frechtman transl. 1947).
6. Exodus 20:3-7.
7. SARTRE, *supra* note 5, at 27.

Ch. 6 Responsibility Toward Fellow Human Beings

infliction of a death sentence in countries where this mode of punishment is recognized, and to killing in a defensive war. The mandate "Thou shalt not steal" might possibly be disobeyed in grave emergencies by a destitute person, provided that the victim of the theft is not seriously hurt by the act.[8] There may be a few situations in which the commission of adultery, contrary to the injunction of the Seventh Commandment, may be defensible. It is more difficult to think of situations in which the directive not to bear false witness against another person might be disregarded for morally persuasive reasons. Conceivably, cases may arise in political trials held in a foreign country when the effect of perjury upon the person or persons directly affected would not be prohibitive, while citizens of the home country of the witness would be placed in serious jeopardy of life or limb by truthful testimony.

The position put forward by Sartre is also subject to criticism. His statement seems to say that we should enter into a choice-requiring situation unarmed with principles of any kind and reach our decision solely in view of the special circumstances of the case. If this anarchic approach is seriously carried through, it might result in many decisions that wreak havoc with the moral and social fabric of a community. Unrestrained selfishness, callousness, and bad faith would have parity of status with conscientious concern for the interests of others as desirable motivations of conduct.

An unconditional recognition of individual moral autonomy would, for example, allow cheating in an exam by a student who believes that success at any price should be the guiding rationale of human actions. It would sanction the commission of arson by one who derives great pleasure from incendiary acts and holds that hedonistic self-satisfaction ought to be the supreme principle of morality. It would authorize dirty tricks, lying, and vilification of an opponent in a political campaign (by asserting falsely, for instance, that he was a psychopath or heroin addict) by a candidate for office who takes the position that acquisition of power should be the sole lodestar in the game of politics.

---

8. An example is the taking of a loaf of bread from someone to feed a starving child, provided that lawful means for obtaining the desperately needed nourishment were not available at the time.

If individualized morality were carried to such extremes, life in society would be permeated by distrust, widespread hostility and a degree of insecurity which would be incompatible with civilized forms of human coexistence. It might be argued that the law could still outlaw antisocial acts which would be within the acceptable range of an individualized morality. But it would be self-contradictory and indefensible to take away by legal prohibitions that which a philosophy of unfettered moral autonomy has bestowed upon human beings as their birthright.

Returning to the position of Sartre, it cannot be assumed that he wished to plead the cause of moral nihilism. It has already been pointed out that he took an extremely broad view of responsibility. "I am responsible for myself and for everyone else."[9] Obviously this means that a person making a decision must consider the effect which this decision will have on other individuals. Sartre even goes a step further. He says:

> To choose to be this or that is to affirm at the same time the value of what we choose, because we can never choose evil. We always choose the good, and nothing can be good for us without being good for all.[10]

While this assertion seems to exhibit an undue degree of optimism concerning the phenomenon of moral choice, it effectively disposes of the assumption that for Sartre good and evil possess equal merit as motives for human action. But his position generally provides little comfort to one seeking illumination in the moral sphere.

C. SITUATION ETHICS

The two alternatives of principled and unprincipled decisionmaking have recently found a complement in a third approach, denominated "situation ethics" by its chief protagonist, Joseph Fletcher. He describes this approach as an

---
9. SARTRE, *supra* note 5, at 21.
10. *Id.* at 20.

intermediate one between norm-guided and individualized morality, although he characterizes it as being closer to the second than the first alternative.[11] Situation ethics recognizes one dominant value which, in Fletcher's opinion, should serve as the touchstone of moral choice: this is the value of love. Love of other human beings, understood in a Christian sense, is to him the only universal and intrinsic good.[12] Its scriptural source is St. Paul's pronouncement "For the whole law is fulfilled in one word, 'You shall love your neighbor as yourself'."[13] All other rules, principles, maxims, and norms are valid only if they happen to serve love in any particular contingency.[14] Situation ethics rejects the notion that, apart from love, the "good" is given in the nature of things; it takes a pragmatic, case-focused view of ethical values other than human benevolence.[15] "The value or worth of anything or any action, in this view, depends upon its circumstances. What is good or right in one context could be evil or wrong in another."[16]

Thus, there exist in situation ethics no general justifications of conduct other than love's expedients. An action which is preponderantly good in light of this criterion may be done, even though the means used to carry it out may entail some evil.[17] The situationist is prepared in any concrete case to suspend, ignore, or violate any principle if by doing so he can effectuate more good than by following it.[18] If a murderer asks a person to divulge his victim's whereabouts, the command that one shall

---

11. J. FLETCHER, MORAL RESPONSIBILITY 168-171, 174 (1967).

It should be mentioned that situation ethics is sometimes identified in linguistic usage with the radically unprincipled morality discussed *supra* under (B).

12. J. FLETCHER, SITUATION ETHICS 30, 64, 68-69, 86 (1966).
13. Gal. 5:14.
14. FLETCHER, *supra* note 12, at 30.
15. *Id.* at 26, 29, 41-42, 64.
16. FLETCHER, *supra* note 11, at 171-172.
17. FLETCHER, *supra* note 12, at 126, 133; FLETCHER, *supra* note 11, at 23.
18. FLETCHER, *supra* note 11, at 31-32.

tell the truth may safely be disregarded.[19] The norm that all deliberate killing of innocent life is wrong may allow of an exception when a person complies with the request of a man hopelessly caught in the burning wreckage of a plane to terminate his life.[20]

The position taken by situation ethics that the only pervasive principle suitable to guide moral choice is the sentiment of love raises more problems than it is capable of solving. It is undoubtedly true that much of the unhappiness existing in this world is produced by the fact that individuals often treat others as objects rather than subjects, paying no attention to their need for concern and respect, and using them as tools for the accomplishment of their own self-regarding purposes. If lovingkindness and unselfishness were practiced on a wide scale, the occurrence of much moral and legal wrong would be avoided.

But it should also be realized that St. Paul's admonition to love your neighbor as yourself does not provide a sufficiently concrete standard for the solution of many problems in which a clash of ethical values occurs. Thus, in the case of the murderer who requests a person cognizant of his intentions to disclose the whereabouts of his would-be victim, the addressee of the request is faced with a conflict between the values of truthfulness and protection of human life. Giving preference to truthfulness would in this instance serve no purpose except dogmatic adherence to a principle, without consideration of consequences. The protection of human life, on the other hand, is a goal entitled to high priority. The principle of love can furnish here no yardstick of decision; its universalization under the theory of situation ethics would entitle both the murderer and his victim to reap its benefits.

The main shortcoming of situation ethics lies in the fact that its justifiable exaltation of love is coupled with an unjustifiable downgrading of all other values to the status of relative and personal maxims of action. Except for love, "there are no values

---

19. FLETCHER, *supra* note 12, at 27. It is well known that Immanuel Kant took the opposite view. I. KANT, CRITIQUE OF PRACTICAL REASON AND OTHER WRITINGS IN MORAL PHILOSOPHY 346-350 (L. Beck ed. 1949).

20. FLETCHER, *supra* note 12, at 75.

at all; there are only things (material and nonmaterial) which *happen* to be valued by persons. This is the personalist view."[21]

This relativization of values leads to a non-directive, wholly individualized ethics in all cases where love and benevolence may be present without supplying a standard for the solution of ethically ambiguous situations. This approach is in many cases not a practicable one. To maintain, as Fletcher does, that the distinction between virtue and vice is largely a matter of personal judgment[22] puts an excessive burden on individuals to resolve issues of good and evil in complex life situations. Such questions are the most difficult ones a person may have to cope with, and reliance on the collective wisdom of the ages is required to aid in their solution.

It is also true that, in the conflict between reason and impulse, there is strong pressure by impulse to rationalize actions highly desired by individuals as good. As a result, situation ethics is likely to produce many actions which are beneficial to the actor but detrimental to others. The overriding command to love your fellowmen will not always alleviate the problem because some ethically relevant decisions will hurt someone while they please another.[23] A person who believes that love for his community warrants the destruction of the reputation and career of a public figure may cause more misery than blessing by his conduct.

Situation ethics may also produce habits which are detrimental to the personal well-being of an individual. For example, someone who recognizes no principles of existential responsibility regarding his own health and social fitness may gradually slip into ever-more dangerous forms of drug addiction.

The drawbacks of situation ethics become highly visible against the background of present-day criminality. The commission of serious crimes has plagued the United States and other countries of the Western World to an ever-increasing extent. A large proportion of such crimes is perpetrated by

---
21. *Id.* at 58. For a criticism of this position see H. BERMAN, THE INTERACTION OF LAW AND RELIGION 81-91 (1974).

22. FLETCHER, *supra* note 12, at 77.

23. A person who leaves his or her spouse to join another loved person may inflict grievous harm on the former.

persons of youthful age. It is widely agreed today that prevention of delinquency is a more effective expedient than punishment after the fact. The experience of countries with low crime rates, such as China and Japan, has shown that an early inculcation of social values is necessary to foster law-abiding conduct. Such education for social fitness cannot be based on a wholly subjective philosophy of basic values. Young people must be taught that acts of violence and spoliation, such as homicide, robbery, arson, and vandalism, are incompatible with unalterable societal needs and will expose the perpetrator to low esteem and deprivations. They should also be instructed that it is everybody's duty to work against the occurrence of such acts and bring them to the attention of the public authorities if their actual or impending commission becomes known to a person. If this type of social teaching takes a firm hold in the minds of the young, peer group pressure will be added to the threat of sanctions in reducing the incidence of antisocial conduct.

D. UNIVERSAL ETHICAL PRINCIPLES

In light of the foregoing observations, it is not surprising that all societies have developed ethical systems with codes containing more than one single supreme principle. Modern anthropology has demonstrated, for example, that all societies have prohibited indiscriminate killing within the group, i.e., killing without some socially relevant justification. All societies have recognized personal property in the goods of consumption and proscribed theft. They have punished incest and rape, although there have been differences in the definition of these offenses. Disadvantageous consequences have been attached to breaches of contract, and at least the grosser forms of fraud have been generally outlawed.[24]

---

24. See Linton, *Universal Ethical Principles: An Anthropological View*, in MORAL PRINCIPLES OF ACTION 645-660 (R. Anshen ed. 1952); Kluckhohn, *Ethical Relativity: Sic et Non*, 52 J. PHILOS. 663 (1955); Mead, *Some Anthropological Considerations concerning Natural Law*, 6 NAT. L. FOR. 51 (1961); Kohlberg, *From Is to Ought*, in COGNITIVE DEVELOPMENT AND EPISTEMOLOGY 155, 174-180 (T. Mischel ed. 1971).

Thus, human beings are universally held responsible for certain types of conduct which are deemed inimical to a workable social order. The fact that a great deal of congruity exists with respect to the practices which are deemed destructive of organized social life cannot be fortuitous. It shows that some basic ethical principles must have their roots in something other than cultural conditioning, namely, in certain traits of human nature that are common to all or most human beings. In the words of Clyde Kluckhohn, "if, in spite of biological variation and historical and environmental diversities, we find these congruences, is there not a presumptive likelihood that these moral principles somehow correspond to inevitabilities, given the nature of the human organism and of the human situation?"[25]

The converging ethical principles (which have often been called principles of "natural law") are not without exceptions, as Linton has shown.[26] Certain forms of intragroup killing are authorized in some societies. In certain Eskimo communities, for example, the duty was imposed on the younger to kill their aged relatives, in order to protect the scarce food supply. In ancient Egypt, the Pharaoh was under obligation to marry his sister, because she alone was deemed equal to him in nobility and biological excellence. Some violations of contract rights and some questionable trade practices bordering on fraud may be permitted by a society, but there is always a limit beyond which one may not go.

Universal ethical principles thus do not constitute absolutes but resemble statistical laws: they hold good in the large majority of instances. Furthermore, refinements in the perception of basic values take place in the course of cultural development; departures from these values regarded as permissible in early civilization may be rejected as opprobrious or cruel at a later stage.[27] While human sacrifices and widow

---
25. Kluckhohn, *supra* note 24, at 675. See also Mead, *supra* note 24, at 53, who speaks of a "minimal culturally transmitted ethical code without which human societies are not viable."
26. Linton, *supra* note 24, at 653-658.
27. Kohlberg, *supra* note 24, at 163-218; Bodenheimer, *Static and Dynamic Natural Law*, 24 OESTERR. ZEITSCHR. F. OEFFENTL. RECHT 13, 16-17 (1973).

burning may be considered justified exceptions from the prohibition of intragroup killing in a developing civilization, such practices will be repudiated as inhuman at a later stage of evolution.

It is the thrust of the foregoing observations that there are some objective universal standards of morality which stem from the natural reactions of human beings to noxious conduct of their fellowmen; the utility of allowing some exceptions from these standards cannot, however, be ruled out *a priori*. All world religions and influential secular creeds have elevated respect for life and personal property, bravery in the face of danger, self-discipline, truthfulness, fairness, and reliability to the rank of positive values. Such values must, as a general rule, be our guides in morally relevant situations. If disregard of a basic value occurs in a case characterized by unusual circumstances, the person or group claiming an exception is saddled with the full burden of proving justification or excuse.

E. CONFLICTS BETWEEN ETHICAL VALUES

Situations arise with some frequency in which clashes arise between two or more values, and where one of them must be given preference in a human decision or action. In such instances, if there is a difference of rank between the values concerned, the lower value should, as a general rule, be sacrificed for the sake of the higher one. Human life and bodily (or mental) integrity normally rank higher on the scale of values than property interests and the obligation to speak the truth.

Suppose, for example, that a woman is near death from a rare disease. There exists one single drug that might save her. It can be procured in only one drugstore in the small town in which the woman lives. The druggist takes advantage of the situation and charges an exorbitant price. There was no time or opportunity for the husband to raise the requisite funds. During the night, he breaks into the store to steal the drug for his wife. Can this action be justified upon the consideration that the value of human life is superior to that of property?

Or suppose that a government withholds news of a disastrous

event which has occurred in the course of a war or serious emergency. Communication of the news might have had a shattering effect upon the morale of the population and armed forces. It might be argued that in this situation the value of preserving public order ought to be given preference over that of truthful news reporting.

The position here proposed differs in some important respects from that of situation ethics. The view that, with the exception of love, all principles, norms, and values are personal and contingent has been rejected as being too subjectivistic and pragmatic. There are some basic values which almost everywhere have been proclaimed to be valid rationales of action. These values should be promoted and their opposing disvalues should be combatted. Where basic values come into conflict, the responsible individual should give priority to those which, in general contemplation, are higher on the measuring scale. Situations may, however, arise in which values of equal rank (such as one human life against another) may be at stake in human decisionmaking. In that event, the choice to be made will not depend on principles or moral norms, but on the exercise of individualized judgment as to which of the available alternatives will produce the greater good or lesser evil. For this category of cases, the propositions enunciated by situation ethics may possess validity.

F. RELATIONS BETWEEN MORAL AND LEGAL RESPONSIBILITY

The relations which exist between these two forms of responsibility may be summarized in four basic propositions. There are areas of social behavior in which moral and legal responsibility coincide, although the exact boundaries of these areas may be subject to change in the course of historical development. There are other fields in which there is some overlapping of these two forms of responsibility, although either one or the other variety is predominant. There are some areas of social conduct which are exclusively within the domain of moral responsibility. There are others which are morally neutral and preempted by legal responsibility.

It has been pointed out earlier in this chapter that one of the principal examples of moral responsibility is the obligation not to harm one's fellow human beings. This obligation is enforced not only by moral pressures applied by the community, but also to a farreaching degree by legal sanctions. It is considered immoral to maim, rob, defraud, swear falsely, and defame. At the same time such acts are criminally prohibited, and the law of torts may also provide civil remedies against offenders.

While there exists a core of common crimes which are almost everywhere and at all times regarded as both immoral and illegal, we also find sectors of social control in which the line between immoral and illegal acts is shifting and subject to historical change. Some of the prohibitions contained in the Ten Commandments may serve as examples. The command that "You shall have no other gods before me"[28] was in the Middle Ages enforced criminally, inasmuch as the advocacy of polytheism was punishable as heresy; this is no longer true in societies which guarantee freedom of religious belief. "Remember the sabbath day to keep it holy"[29] is a moral injunction which in the English-speaking world and some other countries was at one time backed up by penal laws prohibiting commercial and entertainment activities on Sundays; many of these laws have been either repealed or remain unenforced. The command against adultery[30] was in earlier periods not infrequently carried into effect by criminal sanctions, but this happens rarely today in the countries of Western civilization. Homosexual acts between consenting adults have been decriminalized in some European countries where they were at one time proscribed.[31]

Another field in which there exists a wavering line of demarcation between ethical and legal responsibility is unfair competition. Today, many acts done by rivals in business to get an advantage over a competitor are held illegal in the United States; fifty years ago such acts may have been condemned as shabby and unscrupulous without being drawn into the orbit of legal regulation.

---

28. Exodus 20:3.
29. Exodus 20:8.
30. Exodus 20:14.
31. See Richards, *Sexual Autonomy and the Constitutional Right to Privacy*, 30 HAST. L.J. 957, 990 (1979).

The negative moral duty not to injure others is complemented by an affirmative moral obligation to help people in need or distress. This duty is firmly recognized not only by Christianity, but by all leading world religions. For the most part, the obligation to be helpful to others does not lend itself to legal implementation. It would make no sense to pass laws compelling people to dedicate part of their income to private charitable purposes, or to come to the assistance of neighbors who are faced with bothersome inconveniences.

The question arises, however, whether there should be a legal obligation to help a person in obvious peril of life or serious bodily injury, provided it can be done without substantial risk to the would-be rescuer. Suppose a man sees a two-year-old child standing on a railroad track, with a train approaching in the distance; he could lift the child from the track without danger to himself. Or take the case of an employee in a factory who watches a fellow employee with poor eyesight walking into the jaws of a dangerous machine; should he be under a legal duty to warn him? If an accomplished swimmer on a boat deck watches someone drown when he might easily have saved him, would it be unjust to punish him?

There are many countries, in Western Europe as well as in other parts of the world, which recognize a legal duty to aid a person in danger of life, if it can be done without substantial risk to the potential rescuer and third persons. This duty is enforced by penal sanctions, such as a fine or short-term imprisonment, and civil actions in tort against the offender may also be authorized.[32]

The Anglo-American common law has persistently refused to recognize a legal obligation to come to the aid of a person in danger, except in some narrowly delimited situations.[33] For

---

32. See Comment Note, *The Failure to Rescue: A Comparative Study*, 52 COLUM. L. REV. 631 (1952); Feldbrugge, *Good and Bad Samaritans: A Comparative Survey of Criminal Law Provisions Concerning Failure to Rescue*, 14 AM. J. COMPAR. L. 630 (1966).

33. See W. PROSSER, HANDBOOK OF THE LAW OF TORTS 340-343 (4th ed. 1971); Gregory, *The Good Samaritan and the Bad: The Anglo-American Law*, in THE GOOD SAMARITAN AND THE LAW 23-41 (J. Ratcliffe ed. 1966). Among the exceptions from the general rule are: (1) the duty of a ship captain to render assistance to seamen or passengers

example, a motorist who sees a dangerous obstruction on a highway which might cause a serious accident after nightfall is not legally bound to remove it.[34] If a woman becomes ill in a department store and falls to the floor, the store is under no obligation to help her; in the words of a New York court, "the defendant could have let her be and die."[35] A physician is under no duty to answer the call of one who is near death and might be saved.[36]

Jeremy Bentham was shocked by such results and proposed a reform of the law on this question.[37] Many American legal writers have expressed agreement with his position.[38] The moral sense of the community would probably approve the recognition of a legal duty to rescue, provided the duty is made subject to proper limitations. The fact cannot be ignored that the duty of rescue stands in close proximity to the legal obligation to respect the life and bodily integrity of one's fellow human beings. It is clear that one may not violate this obligation by forcible acts of commission. To extend the obligation to situations where life or limb are placed in peril by an omission to act which borders on extreme callousness would involve a relatively small broadening of a general legal principle. If this solution is adopted, the problem of the good samaritan would become one in which there is some overlapping of moral and legal responsibility, although the area as a whole would remain predominantly within the cognizance of morality.

There are also areas of human life which might pose problems of an ethical character to an individual, while the law

---

who are ill or in peril; (2) the duty of motorists to stop and give first aid to those whom they have injured, without regard to questions of fault, as required by statute in many states; and (3) the duty of hosts to invited guests to take reasonable steps to rescue them from perils not created by the negligence of the host.

34. O'Keefe v. W.J. Barry Co., 311 Mass. 517, 42 N.E.2d 267 (1942).
35. Zelenko v. Gimbel Bros. 158 Misc. 904, 287 N.Y.S. 134, 135 (1935).
36. Hurley v. Eddingfield, 156 Ind. 416, 59 N.E. 1058 (1901). For further citations see PROSSER, *supra* note 33, at 341.
37. 1 J. BENTHAM, WORKS 164 (J. Bowring ed. 1962).
38. See the citations in PROSSER, *supra* note 33, at 341, n. 68.

Ch. 6 Responsibility Toward Fellow Human Beings

considers these areas "off limits." The position has been taken in an earlier chapter that morality demands of an individual that he become actually that person which he is potentially.[39] This morality of aspiration can hardly be enforced by legal imperatives. "There is no way by which the law can compel a man to live up to the excellences of which he is capable."[40] It might possibly be argued that compulsory school attendance is designed to assist individuals in their self-improvement. But it would seem that its dominant purpose is a social one. In a complex society, a person without ability to read, write, count, and understand the country's institutions of government and basic rules of social living would be a liability rather than an asset to his community.

Finally, there exist broad areas of the law in which moral valuations do not play any conspicuous part. The technical rules relating to court procedure, the regulations of traffic and transportation, the laws dealing with negotiable instruments belong to this area. The guiding notions of policy in these fields of the law are utility and expediency rather than moral imperatives.

---

39. See *supra* Chapter 4 (A and D).
40. L. FULLER, THE MORALITY OF LAW 9 (rev. ed. 1969).

CHAPTER 7

Social and Political Responsibility

A. SOCIAL RESPONSIBILITY

Under ordinary circumstances, an individual can attain his self-fulfillment only by productive work within a social framework. Most people use their capabilities and special talents in some undertaking that is of benefit to their community or to society at large. They will, with few exceptions, derive a financial remuneration from their work. In return, those who have accepted an assignment or decided to perform a certain task, assume a responsibility for discharging the assignment or task properly and effectively. As was pointed out earlier,[1] social responsibility is rooted in the claims and demands which society makes upon an individual, or an organized group of individuals such as a corporation, when it enlists their participation in socially necessary or useful work.

The law plays a significant role in strengthening and enforcing the social aspects of responsibility. The law of contracts sanctions undertakings and commitments to perform work and services and uses its coercive machinery to secure their performance, if necessary. In some instances, the law allows exceptions from the duty to perform, for example, when performance becomes impossible, without fault of the promisor, due to destruction of a thing to be delivered to the

---
1. See *supra* Chapter 1 (A).

Ch. 7 Social and Political Responsibility 103

other party, or where the purpose of the contract has become totally frustrated by unforeseen events.[2]

The duty of adequate performance is incumbent not only upon individuals contracting to do work for some entrepreneur, but also upon corporate enterprises engaged in supplying goods and services to the public. Thus, a manufacturer of automobiles implicitly promises to sell a safe product fit for use on streets and roads, and a public utility is held accountable to the public for the adequate furnishing of certain services, such as the supply of gas, water, or electricity. A producer of toys assumes responsibility that children will not be injured by their use.

There have in recent times been many complaints that the quality of goods and services furnished to the public has declined in the United States. Reports communicated on television have disclosed that large numbers of cars sold to customers had to be recalled by manufacturers on frequent occasions, because defects affecting their safety had been discovered. A federal commission concluded in 1979 that fifty percent of all repair work done on automobiles was either unnecessary or inadequate.[3] It has also been disclosed that shoddiness of materials or sloppy work in the construction industry has caused damage or inconvenience to the buyers of homes. A news report broadcast on October 3, 1978, stated that the productivity of workers in the United States had gone down sharply and was near the bottom on a worldwide scale.[4] Furthermore, the image of lawyers has suffered because of high fees not always commensurate with the quantity and quality of the work done.[5]

---

2. See J. MURRAY, ON CONTRACTS 388-416 (1974).

3. The gist of the report was communicated by the CBS television network on May 7, 1979.

4. See also Sacramento Bee, February 14, 1979 (p. A-12), reporting a statement made by a Japanese foundation executive to a *Washington Post* reporter to the effect that there was much talk in Japan about the poor quality of many American products.

5. See testimony before the Judiciary Committee of the California Legislature, Sacramento Bee, January 24, 1979. At about the same time, it was reported on television that approximately four billion

If such complaints become widespread, they are liable to have a deleterious effect on the public's confidence in the effectiveness and fairness of the existing social and economic system. The public expects a proper discharge of social responsibility with respect to the adequacy of goods sold and services rendered; in times of rising prices the disappointment suffered by substandard performance is likely to be enhanced. Unless the producers' desire for gain is matched by a general sense of responsibility for putting the quid pro quo for such gain into a craftsmanlike condition, the social order is ultimately headed for trouble. It must also be taken into account that in the area of foreign trade the countries demonstrating superior workmanship will gain an advantage over the United States on the international market. In a more general sense, people will benefit from a recognition of social responsibility because faithful adherence to the principle will enhance the quality of a civilization and the standard of living provided by it. Besides, the individual who lives up to his social responsibility in his work will gain the reward of personal satisfaction with his work and recognition by others.

As far as the legal profession in particular is concerned, it cannot take its present position of power and political influence for granted. The example of ancient Rome, where the guild of lawyers played a role comparable to that of the American legal profession, is instructive. The main charge leveled against private attorneys during the period of the Roman Republic and early Principate was not the size of their fees, but the concentration of their interests on the financial affairs of the wealthy. With the social transformation of the state during the period of the Principate, the influence of wealth declined while the power of governmental bureaucracies increased. In the course of the third and fourth centuries A.D., the legal profession lost much of its political supremacy. The best talents, instead of joining the ranks of private counselors, entered the imperial bureaucracy and became public officials. Legislation and administration, rather than advocacy, became the main concern of the Roman jurists.[6]

---

dollars had been spent during the year 1978 on unnecessary medical operations, and that ten thousand persons had died as a result.

6. See F. SCHULZ, ROMAN LEGAL SCIENCE 262-264 (1946); H. WOLFF, ROMAN LAW 127-130 (1951).

One profession in which exercise of a high degree of responsibility is particularly important is the field of education. Not only the information conveyed by a teacher to his students, but also his personality, conduct, and outlook on life may have a deep impact upon the student's future development. Thorough preparation is, of course, an indispensable precondition of good teaching. Enthusiasm for the subject is also needed, and its presence is not incompatible with an attempt to be fair and objective in discussing matters which go beyond the communication of pure facts. Although the students are entitled to hear the personal opinion of the teacher, he should acquaint them with conflicting positions that might be taken on controversial subjects. Competent analysis of problems does not, however, exhaust the scope of the teacher's responsibility. Behavior on the part of the teacher which breeds cynicism and contempt in the minds of the students will not prepare them well for the pursuit of constructive goals in life. For example, a misuse of a teacher's authority to procure favors from the opposite sex—a practice which appears to have become fairly prevalent in recent times—should be looked upon as an inexcusable violation of professional responsibility.

A California appellate court has held that a high school student has no enforceable right to be taught properly in school.[7] To the extent that the Court denied a tort claim for damages on the part of a student who allegedly had received inadequate instruction, one might go along with the decision. On the other hand, the principle of social responsibility requires that a public school, and the teachers employed by it, must make a maximum effort to prepare the pupils for life by imparting knowledge and basic skills. It would seem that some legal avenue should be provided by which the parents of inadequately instructed students can bring about the removal of clearly incompetent teachers or school administrators.

B. SOCIAL RESPONSIBILITY AND SELF-INTEREST

Social responsibility does not only require the adequate

---

7. Peter W. v. San Francisco Unified School District, 60 Cal. App. 3d 814, 131 Cal. Rptr. 854 (1976).

performance of an assigned or chosen task. It also demands the exercise of restraint in causing disruptions of the public welfare by an unbridled pursuit of self-interest. Classical economic doctrine, as expounded by Adam Smith, assumed that a vigorous striving for gain by each individual would be directed by an invisible hand to the attainment of an end which is in the interest of all.[8] At a time when large numbers of small producers and merchants were in competition with each other, none of them being able to exert a substantial impact on the economic order as a whole, this theory may have carried some persuasive force. The picture changed, however, when important branches of the economy became dominated by large organizations of producers and workers. Under that constellation, an unfettered activation of special group interests in disregard of the common good may have serious, even devastating, consequences.

In 1979, a strike of independent truckers accompanied by violence made it impossible, to a considerable extent, to transport agricultural produce to the centers of distribution. This caused large losses to the suppliers of perishable food products. If carried on for a long time, the strike would have caused serious shortages of goods for the general public. A far-reaching disregard of the general interest, as distinguished from the special interest of a group, raises the question of social responsibility. One major reason for the strike apparently was the high cost and limited availability of diesel fuel. If we assume that the shortage was caused by monopolistic practices to raise the price of the commodity by limiting supply, an issue of social responsibility relating to another group is presented.

Further, the pursuit of self-interest does not justify operations which endanger the health of the public. When an industrial plant, for purposes of economy, recklessly and without warning discharges its refuse into a river which is a source of water supply for the region, Adam Smith's invisible hand will not protect the public from potentially serious injury.

An exercise of social responsibility by industrial and labor organizations is not merely a command of fairness and morality. It is also mandated by the urge for self-preservation. A

---

8. See A. SMITH, THE WEALTH OF NATIONS 326, 423, 594 (Mod. Lib. ed. 1937).

Ch. 7 Social and Political Responsibility

bitter and ruthless struggle between interest groups, and the adoption of policies designed to promote their advantage at the expense of public health and safety, will in the long run jeopardize the very existence of such groups. While a certain amount of vigorous self-assertion and social conflict is inevitable, the pursuit of self-serving practices to the point where the general public is grievously hurt will not remain without consequences for the preservation of a societal order.

C. CONFLICTS BETWEEN MORAL AND SOCIAL RESPONSIBILITY

There are situations in which moral responsibility may part company with social responsibility. Society, or a group within society, may expect of an individual a mode of performing a function which that individual considers contrary to the proper tenets of vocational conduct. A psychiatrist, on grounds of moral or professional integrity, may choose to ignore well-entrenched therapies which he deems contrary to the best interests of his clients. An educator in a country governed by a monolithic ideology may decide to deviate in his teaching from the prescribed orthodoxy, notwithstanding the risk involved, if he cannot reconcile his fundamental beliefs with his society's principles. Such a decision may also open up a gap between social responsibility, as defined by the ruling mores, and a transpersonal responsibility shaped by dedication to cultural values and regarded as superior to these mores.[9]

D. POLITICAL RESPONSIBILITY

Social responsibility takes on a political coloration if the mandate which society entrusts to an individual, or group of individuals, consists in the discharge of governmental functions. In that event, the pertinent type of responsibility is that of a wielder of power toward the persons subject to his authority. In discussing the problem of political responsibility, a distinction must be made between political structures where response to the exercise of political power is tested in periodic

---

9. On transpersonal responsibility see *infra* Chapter 8.

elections offering genuine choices for the electorate, and political systems which do not provide for popular surveillance of a power holder's conduct.

One of the chief temptations incurred by politicians subject to periodic contested elections in a democratic society is the announcement of positions consonant with temporary emotional flareups of public opinion, which may not withstand judicious scrutiny as long-range fundamental objectives. In such a situation, as Walter Lippmann has pointed out, "the decisive consideration is not whether the proposition is good but whether it is popular—not whether it will work well and prove itself but whether the active talking constituents like it immediately."[10] Early in 1979, for example, a senator known for his moderate views made statements on television, obviously in contemplation of a soon-to-begin election campaign, which were apt to inflame public sentiment in favor of reckless external policies. He toned down these extreme statements subsequently in the context of the discussion of specific issues, but not in a manner which was readily recognizable by his audience as inconsistent with his earlier declarations. If such a person wields a strong influence in the formation of policy, conduct of this character may produce consequences which are not really intended by him. The danger is even greater in the case of a leader such as the President of the United States. If for reasons of political expediency he publicly advocates highly dubious measures favored by an incompletely informed electorate, he may ultimately feel compelled to carry them out in order to retain the advantage gained by his earlier policy pronouncements.

Another threat comes to a democratic society from the inclination of opposition leaders to denounce decisions made by the ruling party not on the basis of their merit, but solely for the purpose of discrediting the other side. Here again, the opposition party may become so much identified with the position it has taken that it may feel bound to implement it after coming to power, lest it be charged with deceptive campaigning.

The principle of responsibility clearly requires that deeply-held convictions and positions arrived at rationally on the basis

---

10. W. LIPPMANN, THE PUBLIC PHILOSOPHY 27 (1955).

of the best available evidence should not be sacrificed, in matters important to the well-being of the nation, at the altar of temporary expediency. A political leader in a democratic society must have the courage to forego a continuation of his political career, if such continuation can be bought only at the price of capitulation to fleeting currents of opinion whose victory would in his innermost opinion lead the nation astray. If this principle is not observed, public trust in the worth of public servants is bound to decline. There is a strange paradox in the fact that, although people like their leaders to say what they want to hear, they will lose respect for them if they suspect them of lying for the sake of gaining votes. If deception practiced by public authorities results in serious injuries to members of the public, the scars inflicted on the image of government will be even greater.[11] The fact that barely 37% of the American people went to the polls in the 1978 election bears eloquent testimony to an erosion of confidence in the integrity of the political process and its functionaries.

In non-democratic societies, public officials are confronted with a danger of a somewhat different kind. In these societies, decisions of internal and external policy are usually made by a small group of leaders without previous exposure of the problem to the members of the public. Here the danger does not lie in the making of promises, for purposes of electoral gain, which the makers of the promise know they cannot keep or do not really wish to keep. It rather lies in the temptation to surround all deliberations and decisionmaking processes with complete secrecy and divulge only those facts to the public which the policymakers deem to be consistent with governmental interest. Unless the policies of the government are completely successful in terms of ultimate popular acceptance, the lack of communication between the government and the people, or the maintenance of misleading forms of communication, may gradually sap the confidence of

---

11. When the Atomic Energy Commission conducted nuclear weapons tests in Nevada in the 1950s, the commission knew that some fallout exceeded permissible limits, yet it issued press reports discounting the danger. It claimed falsely that the United States Public Health Service had exonerated fallout as the cause of the death of sheep. Evidence to the effect that large numbers of children had died of leukemia developed later. New York Times, May 1, 1979 (p. A-20).

the people in their rulers. The result may be the growth of disloyalty, decline of morale, and, if the situation deteriorates, sabotage and turmoil. If the servants of a non-democratic society are imbued with a sense of responsibility, they will be governed in their decisions by what they conceive to be the best interests of the populace; at the same time they will maintain a substantial volume of rapport with the people in order to test their reactions to governmental policy.

Whether or not a commonwealth is democratically or nondemocratically organized, the basic criterion of political responsibleness remains the same. The political leaders of a country should strive to promote the common good, i.e., the interest of the whole as opposed to the interest of special privileged groups. Since political, social, and economic conditions change, and with them the problems engendered by these conditions, it is not possible to give a definition of the public interest with a concrete, normative content. Walter Lippmann has said that "the public interest may be presumed to be what men would choose if they saw clearly, thought rationally, acted disinterestedly and benevolently."[12] This formulation addresses itself to the attitude and state of mind required for arriving at sound decisions of public policy; it does not suggest a substantive yardstick applicable at all times for determining the requirements of the public good.[13]

E. HUMAN RIGHTS AND CIVIC OBLIGATIONS

It would seem clear that, in a modern civilized state, one of the essential criteria for serving the public good is the recognition and protection of basic human rights by the government. The need for recognizing such rights is anchored deeply in the fabric of the human personality. First of all, people desire a substantial amount of freedom. They do not

---

12. LIPPMANN, *supra* note 10, at 42.
13. For a more concrete analysis of the public interest by this author see E. BODENHEIMER, JURISPRUDENCE: THE PHILOSOPHY AND METHOD OF THE LAW 240-245 (rev. ed. 1974); Bodenheimer, *Prolegomena to a Theory of the Public Interest*, in THE PUBLIC INTEREST 205-217 (NOMOS vol. V, C. Friedrich ed. 1962).

Ch. 7 Social and Political Responsibility

wish to be forcibly confined to places which are not of their choice, or to be restrained from unobjectionable actions which they consider conducive to their interests; they also desire to pursue their life aims in a social context which affords them the opportunity of self-actualization. Secondly, people strive for a reasonable amount of equality. They do not wish to be subject to the arbitrary power of others who use them purely as tools for their own subjective purposes; they are also opposed to unequal treatment based on irrelevant grounds for the differentiation. Thirdly, people desire to be protected against attacks which menace their life, bodily integrity, or property; in other words, they strive for a certain amount of security. In a modern developed society, people also wish to live in reasonably decent surroundings, acquire some amount of knowledge, and be supplied with facilities for maintaining and improving their health.

The fact that people desire certain things does not, of course, prove irrefutably that they ought to desire them. If most men, for example, should wish to have ten wives, this does not demonstrate a social necessity for permitting polygamy. The general penchant for the rights referred to above, on the other hand, mirrors human aspirations which a rational analysis of the human condition must adjudge to be justified. The quest for rights of freedom, equality, and security, as well as the desire for opportunities of work, recreation, education, and health care are conducive to the development of productive personalities and thus serve the interests of society. A responsible government will therefore do everything in its power to insure that these rights are implemented to the maximum extent consistent with social realities.

A grant of basic human rights to the members of a community or state would be meaningless unless it is coupled with the recognition and enforcement of obligations. A right is an entitlement conferred upon an individual to do something, refrain from doing something, or receive certain benefits. The grant of a right does not *per se* insure respect by the grantee for the equal rights accorded to others. A responsible government will therefore not only secure the rights of individuals but at the same time insist on compliance with legal obligations which the bearers of rights have toward other persons or the community at large.

The common good, which must be the lodestar of responsible government, imposes tasks of great diversity and complexity upon the officers of the state. If the exercise of a right becomes incompatible with the original purpose for which the right was granted, some legal limitations upon the use of the right may become necessary. Thus vicious and slanderous denunciations of an opponent in a political campaign are not consonant with the purpose of political free speech to further the rational and multifaceted discussion of public issues. The use of private property in a manner which produces a serious health hazard for the neighborhood clearly does not serve the public interest. The endeavor of the public authorities to reconcile and adjust conflicting rights and interests will not in all cases lead to an optimum result satisfactory to all concerned. The principle of responsible discharge of public functions demands, however, that feasible alternatives be carefully considered. An effort must be made to find a solution which does not give priority to one particular interest over equally legitimate interests for ulterior motives unrelated to the merits of the issue at stake.

F. POWER AND RESPONSIBILITY

A statement to the effect that the chief duty of governing authorities is a conscientious and responsible attitude toward the governed has the ring of a commonplace truth. Such a statement would certainly reflect the view of the overwhelming majority of men and women in any part of the world. But in past and present political theory, the proper discharge of governmental functions is by no means generally defined in terms of responsibility toward the people. In classical antiquity the sophist Thrasymachus, according to Plato's rendition of his views, considered government coterminous with a maximum effort to secure benefits for the rulers.[14] In the early twentieth century, the Italian political scientist Gaetano Mosca declared that a ruling class is characterized by the fact that it monopolizes power and enjoys the advantages that power confers; he did concede, however, that such enjoyment might be shortlived unless the exercise of material and intellectual force

---
14. PLATO, THE REPUBLIC, Bk. I. 338-339 (Everyman's Lib. ed. 1950).

was tempered by adherence to some moral principles.[15] His contemporary Vilfredo Pareto was less impressed with the need of ruling groups to pay attention to what he called "the humanitarian doctrine." A government moving in the direction of this doctrine is, in his words, "less and less capable of using force and is so shirking the main duty of a ruling class."[16] The rejection of the idea that the welfare of the people is the objective of government reached its apogee in the philosophy of Friedrich Nietzsche. He maintained that the leaders of a nation had the right to sacrifice human beings, not in the service of an idea, but simply for the purpose of strengthening their power and enjoying it to the fullest.[17]

The idea that power rather than social responsibility is the lodestar of politics still finds adherents in present-day political theory. A well-known political scientist, Karl Loewenstein, has said: "Politics is nothing else but the struggle for power."[18] Harold Lasswell has declared: "The study of politics is the study of influence and the influential . . . . The influential are those who get the most of what there is to get."[19] Hans Morgenthau, who is primarily interested in international affairs, has argued that the aim of international politics is "either to keep power, to increase power, or to demonstrate power."[20] All the authors mentioned seem to assume that they are describing a permanent and inevitable attribute of the political principle. They exhibit no interest in a normative theory of politics pointing in a different direction.

It would, of course, be a mistake to underestimate the role of power in the conduct of national and international affairs. No internal program of social improvement or legal reform can be carried out effectively unless the person or body executing the

---

15. G. MOSCA, THE RULING CLASS 50, 71 (A. Livingston ed. 1939).
16. V. PARETO, 3 THE MIND AND SOCIETY 1293; 4 *id.* 1532 (A. Livingston ed. 1935).
17. 14 F. NIETZSCHE, GESAMMELTE WERKE 209 (Musaron ed. 1925).
18. K. LOEWENSTEIN, POLITICAL POWER AND THE GOVERNMENTAL PROCESS 3 (1957).
19. H. LASSWELL, POLITICS: WHO GETS WHAT, WHEN, HOW? 13 (1958).
20. H. MORGENTHAU, POLITICS AMONG NATIONS 36 (4th ed. 1967).

program possess the power of achieving its goals. A nation active in international affairs will be unable to pursue its external political and economic objectives if it lacks the power of successful action.

There is, however, a fundamental distinction between power understood as an instrumental value and power conceived as an ultimate goal. This distinction has been emphasized particularly by Bertrand Russell and Martin Buber. Russell has stated: "Love of power, if it is to be beneficent, must be bound up with some end other than power."[21] The purpose for exercising power, he argued, must be one which is in harmony with the desires of people who will be significantly affected if the purpose is realized. Martin Buber, in contrast to Morgenthau, was convinced that:

> Greatness strives neither to "increase" nor to "display" power. The great man ... is powerful, involuntarily and composedly powerful, but he is not avid for power. What he is avid for is the realization of what he has in mind, the incarnation of the spirit. Of course he needs power for this realization; for power—when we strip the concept of the dithyrambic splendor with which Nietzsche equipped it—means simply the capacity to realize what one wants to realize; but the great man is not avid for this capacity—which is, after all, only a self-evident and indispensable means—but for *what* he wishes to be capable of .... When we see a great man desiring power instead of his real goal we soon recognize that he is sick, or more precisely that his attitude to his work is sick.[22]

The question arises, of course, whether such statements represent purely subjective and emotional reactions rather than enunciations of a higher truth capable of verification. It is submitted that the views expressed by Russell and Buber can find a great deal of corroboration in psychological and sociological facts.

First of all, the experience of many centuries has shown that there is a strain of idealism in most healthy individuals which

---
21. B. RUSSELL, POWER: A NEW SOCIAL ANALYSIS 264 (1938).
22. M. BUBER, BETWEEN MAN AND MAN 151 (1965).

makes them wish to take on, or fight for, a cause they deem worthwhile.[23] We have the testimony of a hard-boiled realist, the Emperor Napoleon, in support of this view. He wrote in 1808: "In war, moral factors account for three quarters of the whole; relative material strength accounts for only one quarter."[24] The validity of this statement was corroborated by his own experience as a military leader. His army put up a superb fight during his early campaigns, when the spirit of the French Revolution was still strong and Napoleon was generally considered the executor of the aims of this revolution. At later stages of his career, Napoleon became intoxicated with power and played a somewhat cynical game of politics. He did so, first, in the favoritism shown to his brothers in the creation of new dynasties in countries subdued by France, and secondly, in his marriage of convenience to a member of Austrian royalty. There is much reason to believe that these events dampened the morale of his soldiers and contributed to Napoleon's ultimate defeat.

In the internal affairs of a nation, a philosophy which views the area of political and economic activity as a happy hunting ground for the privileged few tends to breed dissension, factional strife, and ultimate social turmoil. For this reason and others, no political party has ever proclaimed the purpose of government to be the satisfaction of the needs of an elite, and no philosopher of rank has subscribed to this view. Even Nietzsche, who went further than probably any other thinker in treating the interests of the majority with disdain, argued that a prudent group of rulers will normally grant rights to the people in order to construct a safer base for its power. But values such as liberty, equality, and general security were to him primarily "flags" used for reasons of political advantage to disguise the real power aims of the dominant group.[25] He extended his

---

23. See E. FROMM, THE SANE SOCIETY 29 (1955): "All men are idealists and cannot help being idealists, provided we mean by idealism the striving for the satisfaction of needs which are specifically human and transcend the physiological needs of the organism." See also V. FRANKL, THE DOCTOR AND THE SOUL 7, 55 (1971).
24. THE MIND OF NAPOLEON 219 (J. Herold ed. 1955).
25. 10 F. NIETZSCHE, GESAMMELTE WERKE 101 (Musarion ed. 1925); F. NIETZSCHE, THE WILL TO POWER 50 (W. Kaufmann ed. 1968).

power philosophy to the international field without, however, advocating the perpetuation of nationalism as the primary incentive of international life. He spoke of the future "rulers of the world," a highly disciplined aristocracy whose task it would be to fashion a universal order and to set a new pattern of values for humanity.[26]

Today, the world is fragmented by the ideological struggle of nations and the tensions between the superpowers. Whatever the ultimate outcome of this struggle, it seems clear to all reasonable persons that the main goal of international politics must be the building of a world in which wholesale destruction of mankind is rendered impossible.[27] This aim cannot in the long run be made subservient to any other aim, especially not to a philosophy which considers enhancement of national power as the *ultima ratio* and final goal of international relations.

If this premise is accepted, one must agree with Romano Guardini that in the coming epoch—with the probable exception of a turbulent transition period—the essential problem will not be that of increasing power but of curbing it. The core of the new epoch's intellectual task will be to integrate power into life in such a way that human beings can employ power without forfeiting their humanity.[28] What this means is that power must be translated into responsibility for the preservation and well-being of mankind.

Is this a utopian dream? Is it possible to imbue those who stand at the top of the societal ladder with the conviction that power is merely an instrument for the attainment of aims which negate the will to power as a primary determinant of social action? It cannot be doubted that there have been statesmen, such as Pericles, Marcus Aurelius, Frederick the Great of Prussia, Jefferson, Lincoln, and others, whose policies were guided by a desire to promote the common good rather than by a wish to use and augment their personal power. It should become the task of political education to inculcate a similar attitude in the statesmen of the future.

---

26. NIETZSCHE, THE WILL TO POWER, *supra* note 25, at 504, 519.
27. See in this connection I. TAMMELO, SURVIVAL AND SURPASSING 50-51, 124-125 (1971).
28. R. GUARDINI, POWER AND RESPONSIBILITY xiii (1961).

G. ANONYMITY OF RESPONSIBILITY

In Franz Kafka's novel *The Castle*, the leading figure has supposedly been hired as a land surveyor by a governmental organization housed in a castle. After arriving in the adjacent town, he attempts to find out whether and in what manner he should start his activities. He is unsuccessful in locating and speaking to the official who can answer his questions, and he receives inconsistent information from various units in the castle. Kafka makes the following observation: "It may happen in a large governmental machinery that one department ordains this, another that: neither knows of the other."[29] The inability to pierce the anonymity of a bureaucratic system constitutes a rather frequent occurrence in modern times.

A similar problem exists in the context of corporate enterprise. Responsibility in such an enterprise, when it is large enough, is widely dispersed, and often a search for the party in the corporate hierarchy who should account for an act or omission is unavailing.

Legislatures have sometimes attempted to circumvent the problem of identification by penalizing the corporate body as such for illegal actions by the imposition of monetary fines. This is a questionable solution in most cases, since such an expense will normally be treated as a cost of doing business; it will ultimately be borne either by the stockholders by way of decreased dividends or by the general public by means of increased prices. The parties that should be subjected to the sanctions of the criminal law are those corporate functionaries who either intended the harm attributed them or were negligent in causing it.[30]

The pressures exercised by special interest groups on government pose another problem of tracing responsibility to its actual source. If an interest group wields great economic power or controls important natural resources, it may be able to force government into actions which in effect carry out the

---
29. F. KAFKA, THE CASTLE 77 (W.&E. Muir ed. 1954).
30. See E. BODENHEIMER, TREATISE ON JUSTICE 202-210 (1967); Allen, Comment, 23 U. MICH. L. QUADR. NOTES 5 (No. 1, 1978).

decisions of private organizations. In such cases, it is common for the majority of the people to blame the government for an action which really was not its own.[31] Even where an economic event, such as shortage of a commodity or increase of price, can clearly be traced to a determinate source, as for instance the oil industry, it will often be difficult for the public, including its elected representatives, to obtain the data necessary to form a fair judgment.

The question must also be raised whether the head of a government department, or the chief of a bureau, should be held responsible for all derelictions of duty occurring within the department or bureau. The same question arises in the context of a military establishment. Should a commanding general, for example, be made to answer for atrocities committed by inferior officers or soldiers, of which he had no knowledge?[32] The position has been taken in this book that a violation of responsibility implies some degree of blameworthy conduct.[33] If we adhere to this principle, we should limit imputation of liability to cases in which the top official was chargeable at least with negligence in selecting or supervising the subordinates guilty of serious misconduct, or in failing to issue instructions which might have prevented such misconduct.

Problems of a special nature in locating political responsibility arise in the international field. When the American Ambassador to Afghanistan was killed in 1979 in a shootout between police and rebels who had kidnapped him, the American Government first blamed the incident on Russian advisers to the Afghan Government who, in the opinion of the State Department, had not sufficiently counseled restraint. Later the Department referred to the possibility that some subordinate Afghan official might have been responsible for the killing. The power of observing and tracing events occurring in a foreign country is often quite limited.

---

31. See in this connection the instructive observations by H. EHRMANN, ORGANIZED BUSINESS IN FRANCE 271-276 (1957).

32. This was the problem posed at the trial of General Yamashita for war crimes committed in the Philippine Islands during World War II. See A. REEL, THE CASE OF GENERAL YAMASHITA (1971).

33. See *supra* Chapter 1 (B).

Ch. 7 Social and Political Responsibility

In the atomic age, the most appalling danger to the human race is posed by the potential misuse or careless use of atomic power. Even when the top layers of government are conscious of their responsibility for the survival of mankind, a mistake or unauthorized act on the part of subordinate officials always remains within the range of possibility. This raises the specter of war engendered by misunderstandings which may not be amenable to timely rectification. If that happens, the issue of ultimate responsibility may become so clouded by rapidly moving events that the historians of a later age may be at a loss to unravel the mystery.

CHAPTER 8

Transpersonal Responsibility

A. THE BENEFITS OF CIVILIZATION-BUILDING

Transpersonal responsibility is a special variety of social responsibility which involves dedication to impersonal values rather than the commitment of individuals and organizations to perform work or services. This form of responsibility comprises above all the promotion of values which relate to the creation and maintenance of a rich and flourishing civilization.

The term "civilization" is used here in a broad sense which includes the material as well as the spiritual side of mankind's productive activity. Some authors have assigned a narrower meaning to the concept. Spengler and MacIver, for example, have reserved the term civilization to those human efforts in the realm of technology and practical science which are directed toward increasing the variety, quantity, and quality of material goods. Improvements in the construction of buildings, inventions of new machines, advancements in efficient methods for producing automobiles and airplanes would thus be viewed as accomplishments of civilization. The word "culture" is used by these authors to designate the creative achievements of the human mind in the areas of art, music, literature, philosophy, and religion.[1]

---

1. See 1 O. SPENGLER, THE DECLINE OF THE WEST 31-32, 104-108, 354-355 (1926); R. MACIVER, SOCIETY: ITS STRUCTURE AND CHANGES 225-226 (1932).

There are other authors, however, who have treated civilization and culture as coterminous notions which refer to a society's way of life in all of its manifestations.[2] The discussion which follows will draw no sharp distinction between civilization and culture, but it will generally limit the term culture to the nontechnical aspects of civilization, such as the fine arts and reflective thinking on meanings and values.

The German legal philosopher Joseph Kohler has said: "Human activity is cultural activity. Man's task is to create and develop culture, to obtain permanent cultural values, thus producing a new abundance of forms which shall be as a second creation, in juxtaposition to divine creation."[3] Using the term culture in a comprehensive sense, Kohler asserted that the promotion of culture was not only one of the tasks, but *the* task of mankind.[4] While issue might be taken with this sweeping statement, there is great merit in the assumption that civilization-building is, or should be, mankind's chief concern.

Certain facets of civilization are indispensable for producing the minimum conditions for a bearable form of human life. Over and above these most essential aspects of social order arise those cultural activities which make life fuller, richer, and more worthwhile. The archaeologists tell us that already in primitive society sculptures appear which are often engraved on rocks or similar formations. Music is found as an important segment of life in very early communities, and religion with the monuments and rites which form part of it has had a long history in all countries of the world.

Gustav Radbruch has said that history has always judged nations and peoples by the contributions they have made to culture and civilization.[5] There is a great deal of truth in this observation. If a society fosters in its members the full

---

2. 1 B. TYLOR, PRIMITIVE CULTURE 1 (1958); B. MALINOWSKI, A SCIENTIFIC THEORY OF CULTURE 36 (1944). For a comprehensive survey of conflicting viewpoints see A. KROEBER & C. KLUCKHOHN, CULTURE: A CRITICAL REVIEW OF CONCEPTS AND DEFINITIONS (1952).

3. J. KOHLER, PHILOSOPHY OF LAW 4 (A. Albrecht transl. 1914).

4. *Ibid.* Kohler included in his definition of culture aesthetic culture, knowledge, and the technical control of nature. *Id.* at 22.

5. Radbruch, *Legal Philosophy*, in THE LEGAL PHILOSOPHIES OF LASK, RADBRUCH, AND DABIN 97 (K. Wilk transl. 1950).

development of all the multifarious powers and capacities possessed by human beings, if it works toward the perfection of individuals and the social institutions serving them, such a society will call forth the admiration of contemporary and future generations, inside as well as outside the particular society.

The civilization of ancient Greece provides a good example. The leading Greek philosophers, and especially Plato and Aristotle, have not only been a source of inspiration for large numbers of thinkers in many countries and in all subsequent periods of history; their teachings have actually influenced the conduct of life of innumerable persons, including many who had never heard the names of these men. The spread of Neoplatonism in the late Roman Empire prepared the ground for the acceptance of Christianity by large masses of people. Many elements of Aristotelian philosophy entered into the imposing edifice of thought produced by St. Thomas Aquinas, whose doctrines became part of the world view proclaimed by the Roman Catholic Church. The dynamic philosophy of Heracleitus, especially his apothegm "Everything is in a state of flux," gave impetus to dialectical thinking and historical evolutionism, two related modes of thought which did not remain confined to a small intellectual elite but entered significantly into the ideology of mass movements such as Marxism.

Untold numbers of people have derived enjoyment from the great works of art produced by the Greeks, especially in the field of sculpture. Some of the plays written by Aeschylus, Sophocles, and Euripides, which attracted large crowds to the amphitheaters of Greece, are still being performed on the stage in many countries. Political science and political practice have profited from the first successful experiment in democracy consummated in ancient Athens.

Greek culture is only a microcosm in the worldwide universe of civilization. It would take many volumes to write up the global history of civilization in its most outstanding achievements. Such a history, if it refuses to be selective, would have to include the progress made in the natural sciences, which are also a product of the sharpening and refinement of the human spirit that accompanies a developing civilization. Large numbers of individuals have found their place in life by analyzing and evaluating the contributions made by great philosophers, scientists, jurists, artists, and writers, and by performing the works of dramatists and composers. Academic institutions would be nonexistent if human life were conducted on a primitive, brutelike level. Furthermore, millions of people have experienced an enrichment of their lives by traveling to countries or cities which harbor treasures of civilization, such as beautiful buildings, churches, museums, and monuments of the past, or which afford their visitors delectations in their theatres, opera houses, or concert halls.

B. SKEPTICAL VIEWS ON CIVILIZATION-BUILDING

The foregoing account of the benefits of civilization might sound commonplace and trite were it not for the fact that in the present century some downgrading of cultural pursuits and the life of the spirit has taken place. The anticultural bias can be traced back to Nietzsche, although it does not express itself in his writings in the form of a frontal assault. It does manifest itself in many open and disguised suggestions by this philosopher that biological values are superior to spiritual values. In Heidegger's authoritative interpretation, a human being is to Nietzsche essentially a jumble of bodily desires and irrational impulses. "By going back to the body as the metaphysical clue, all interpretation of the world is carried out [by Nietzsche]."[6] For example, thinking is defined by Nietzsche as a "relation of our drives to each other."[7] Referring to this statement, Heidegger concludes that thinking and reason are reduced by Nietzsche to the service of "animality."[8]

A disciple of Nietzsche, Ludwig Klages, carried the views of the philosopher to a more extreme conclusion by proclaiming

---

6. 2 M. HEIDEGGER, NIETZSCHE 190 (1961) [My translation].
7. F. NIETZSCHE, *Beyond Good and Evil*, in BASIC WRITINGS OF NIETZSCHE 237 (W. Kaufmann ed. 1968); See also 16 F. NIETZSCHE, GESAMMELTE WERKE 65 (Musarion ed. 1925): "Thinking is a sign language concerning the power balance between impulses." [My translation].
8. HEIDEGGER, *supra* note 6, at 294.

that life and the spirit were irreconcilable antagonists.[9] In the opinion of Klages, a human being "sicklied o'er with the pale cast of thought"[10] will inhibit and damage his vital forces by indulging in the cultivation of the spirit. When we confront this assertion with the uncontestable statement by the geneticist Dobzhansky that "man became a winner in the evolutionary race because of the powers of his brain, not those of his body,"[11] it becomes clear what consequences an acceptance of Klages' theory would have for the future of civilization.

The trend of thinking implicit in the work of Klages was taken up and intensified by certain reinterpreters of Freudian psychoanalysis, especially Géza Róheim and Norman Brown. These writers saw a sign of neurosis in any subordination of bodily, especially sexual, interests to the purely spiritual side of human activity. Róheim bluntly asserted the "structural and fundamental identity of neurosis and civilization."[12] Brown declared that "knowledge is carnal knowledge," that "the body that is the measure of all things is sexual," and that "the aim of psychoanalysis . . . is to return our souls to our bodies."[13]

C. THE FREUDIAN POSITION

Freud's own position toward the value of civilization was ambivalent. On the one hand, he believed that civilization has been created at the cost of reduced satisfaction of basic instincts, especially the sexual instinct and the impulse of aggression. With reference to the sexual instinct, he expressed the view that its taming and partial repression was essential to the maintenance of civilized conditions of life.[14] In this respect, he said, "civilization is obeying the laws of economic necessity,

---

9. L. KLAGES, DER GEIST ALS WIDERSACHER DES LEBENS 69, 253, 435 (4th ed. 1960).

10. W. SHAKESPEARE, HAMLET, Act III, Sc. 1.

11. Dobzhansky, *Human Nature as a Product of Evolution*, in NEW KNOWLEDGE OF HUMAN VALUES 78 (A. Maslow ed. 1959).

12. G. RÓHEIM, THE ORIGIN AND FUNCTION OF CULTURE 24 (1943).

13. N. BROWN, LOVE'S BODY 249, 265 (1966); N. BROWN, LIFE AGAINST DEATH 158 (1959).

14. S. FREUD, THE COMPLETE INTRODUCTORY LECTURES ON PSYCHOANALYSIS 311 (J. Strachey transl. 1971).

since a large amount of the psychical energy which it uses for its own purposes has to be withdrawn from sexuality."[15] This process of withdrawal he called "sublimation of instinct," and he asserted that it was the source and indispensable prerequisite of all scientific, artistic, and ideological activities.[16]

This partial displacement of libido by a process of sublimation for the sake of cultural aims was responsible, in Freud's opinion, for a great deal of frustration and suffering among human beings; their physical and psychic structure, he maintained, was not well adapted to the sacrifice of primary instincts.[17] A suppression of such instincts, in his opinion, is apt to produce neurotic symptoms in human beings and, more significantly, to create hostility against the conditions of civilization.[18] In light of these facts, Freud raised the question whether we might not be justified in reaching the conclusion that some civilized societies, and possibly the whole of civilized mankind, have become "neurotic."[19]

There are, on the other hand, passages in Freud's work which indicate that he was by no means an enemy of civilization, and that he considered the instinctual deprivations required for its maintenance a necessary price for the blessings it bestows upon the human race. He said, for example, that the impulses which are diverted from their sexual aims and directed to cultural purposes are "socially higher."[20] He also stated that the pleasures derived by an artist from his creative achievements, and those of a scientist discovering a new truth had a "special quality," and that we are justified in characterizing these pleasures as "finer and higher" than purely sensual gratifications.[21] He ended his discussion of the relation between

---

15. S. FREUD, CIVILIZATION AND ITS DISCONTENTS 51 (J. Strachey transl. 1961).
16. *Id.* at 44.
17. *Id.* at 26-27. For this reason, Norman O. Brown did not only reject the path of sublimation, but found an "intrinsic insanity" in its practice. BROWN, LIFE AGAINST DEATH 307, 158 (1959).
18. FREUD, *supra* note 15, at 34, 44. See also S. FREUD, THE FUTURE OF AN ILLUSION 3, 19 (J. Strachey transl. 1964).
19. FREUD, *supra* note 15, at 91.
20. FREUD, *supra* note 14, at 23.
21. FREUD, *supra* note 15, at 26.

libidinal satisfaction and cultural progress by declaring that as an impartial scientist he wished to refrain from expressing an opinion upon the value of civilization. He vouched that he could listen without indignation to the critic who doubted that the whole enterprise was worth the trouble and suffering which it entailed. At the same time he expressed understanding for the person who was convinced of the imperative necessity of civilization, and who took the position that the tendencies toward a restriction of sexual life required for its preservation and growth should be taken in their stride with serenity.[22] In another work, he went a step further by stating that the abolition of civilization would be "short-sighted," because a state of nature characterized by an unrestrained roaming of human impulses and passions would be unbearable.[23] He suggested at the same time that the demands for instinctual renunciation made by the society of his own time were probably excessive, and that their stringency could be reduced.[24]

D. SEX AND CULTURAL ACHIEVEMENT

The Freudian theory concerning the relation between sex and culture was put to an empirical test by a British scholar, Joseph Daniel Unwin. He conducted a large-scale investigation into the sex regulations of eighty uncivilized societies and a number of historically advanced societies, such as the Sumerian, Babylonian, Greek, Roman, Moorish, and English cultures. The conclusion he arrived at was that the amount of cultural ascent in the eighty primitive societies paralleled the degree of limitation which these societies placed upon sexual opportunities. He also noted that all advanced societies, with the exception of Islamic civilization, were organized on the basis of monogamy, a form of sexual regulation which, if enforced by the moral code of a society with some degree of effectiveness, entails a decrease of sexual opportunities.[25]

More specifically, Unwin found that those few societies

---

22. *Id.* at 91-92.
23. FREUD, THE FUTURE OF AN ILLUSION, *supra* note 18, at 20.
24. FREUD, *supra* note 15, at 62, 90.
25. J. UNWIN, SEX AND CULTURE 374, 382 (1934).

which imposed no restraints at all on sexual activity developed no art, literature, or philosophical reflection; they were unable even to build monuments to religion, such as temples. Those societies which enforced a modicum of continence created a measure of culture, though on a relatively modest level. The group of societies which maintained the custom of monogamous marriage in a by-and-large effective form and over a prolonged period of time attained the highest position on the cultural scale. This, according to him, is due to the fact that legal and moral curbs on the sexual impulse tend to produce thought, reflection, and social energy. The loosening of restrictions on sexual activity, on the other hand, has always led, in his opinion, to a gradual decrease of cultural achievements.[26] His basic thesis is summarized in the following statement: "A limitation of sexual opportunity always is, and as far as I know always has been accompanied by a rise in cultural condition, but from a bare study of the facts alone it is impossible for me to say that the coincidence is inevitable."[27]

Unwin's intimation that a society must make a choice between the enjoyment of sexual freedom and the boon of cultural flowering will be questioned by many. Thus far, however, it has not been refuted by convincing evidence, and it is fully in consonance with the findings of Freud. Freud maintained that civilization is the product of a partial repression of the sexual instinct; the logic of his thought leads to the conclusion that, on an overall basis, the volume of energy released for cultural purposes is roughly proportional to the degree of instinctual restraint.[28] Unwin's thesis was accepted by the historian Arnold Toynbee and the sociologist Pitirim Sorokin, and it has received support from certain conclusions in the Kinsey report.[29]

Some corroboration of the thesis is provided by a comparison of the achievements of ancient civilization with those of the Judaeo-Christian civilization. The ascetic strain in ethics,

---
26. *Id.* at 13-14, 23-32, 83-84, 317-318.
27. *Id.* at 2.
28. See *supra* under (C).
29. See V. PACKARD, THE SEXUAL WILDERNESS 420-425 (1968), with citations.

which is already noticeable in the moral exhortations of the Jewish prophets, became very strong in the teachings of the Christian churches, particularly in the Middle Ages. It was for the most part absent in the civilization of the Greeks and Romans. Although monogamy was the official form of sexual union in ancient Greece, relations with cultivated courtesans called *hetaerae* were common and not repudiated by public opinion. The general availability of slaves of both sexes added greatly to the volume of sexual opportunity. In Rome, the relative austerity of morals in the early and republican periods gave way to a time of free-wheeling sexual indulgence during the first two centuries after the birth of Christ.[30]

The denunciation of sexual license found in the New Testament, especially in the epistles of Paul, was a reaction to the conditions which prevailed in the Roman Empire. The pendulum then swung all the way from acceptance of well-nigh complete sexual freedom to a hostile attitude toward sex as divorced from procreation. Carnal indulgence for its own sake was a sin in the view of Paul.[31] It is good for a man not to touch a woman, he said.[32] Celibacy and virginity were held superior in ethical rank to the married state; it was logical from this point of view to impose celibacy upon the priesthood. Marriage was recognized as a necessity for the majority of people, but sexual activity unassociated with procreative purposes was, as a matter of general principle, viewed with disfavor by leading church fathers and influential theologians.[33] According to St. Thomas Aquinas, the renunciation of bodily pleasures is more pleasing in the sight of God than the enjoyment of it.[34]

---

30. For elaborate descriptions see 1 L. FRIEDLAENDER, DARSTELLUNGEN AUS DER SITTENGESCHICHTE ROMS 481-509 (1910); O. KIEFER, SEXUAL LIFE IN ANCIENT ROME (1934).

31. Rom. 7:14-25; 8:6-9.

32. 1 Corint. 7:1.

33. *Id.* at 7:2, 8-9, 32-34, 38. This position was generally shared by other church authorities. See H. VON EICKEN, GESCHICHTE UND SYSTEM DER MITTELALTERLICHEN WELTANSCHAUUNG 123-124 (1887); 1 J. MAUSBACH, DIE ETHIK DES HEILIGEN AUGUSTINUS 250, 357 (1909).

34. ST. THOMAS AQUINAS, SUMMA THEOLOGICA, Pt. II (First Part), Qu. 34, Art. 1; Qu. 72, Art. 2; Qu. 73, Art. 7; Qu. 74, Arts. 3 and 4 (Fathers of the English Dominican Province transl. 1927). See also W. COLE, SEX IN CHRISTIANITY AND PSYCHOANALYSIS 80 (1955).

Ch. 8 Transpersonal Responsibility

Protestantism abolished celibacy for the priesthood. It also rejected the medieval position that chastity was *per se* superior to its opposite. Luther said that "one has to have the heart for chastity, otherwise all such things are worse than hell and purgatory."[35] He also taught, contrary to medieval doctrine, that "before God a married woman is better than a virgin."[36] On the other hand, he declared categorically that God does not want sex outside of marriage.[37] While he was not in favor of monastic asceticism, he believed in the superior value of a life devoted to hard work and guided by strong control over the desires.

Calvin's position was similar to Luther's.[38] Max Weber has given us a penetrating analysis of the secular asceticism inherent in the Calvinistic Puritan tradition.[39] He said:

> The sexual asceticism of Puritanism differs only in degree, not in fundamental principle, from that of monasticism; and on account of the Puritan conception of marriage, its practical influence is more far-reaching than that of the latter. For sexual intercourse is permitted, even within marriage, only as a means willed by God for the increase of His glory according to the commandment, 'Be fruitful and multiply.'[40]

The end of life, according to this religious conception, is hard work in a person's calling, and not the maximization of pleasure. In Weber's view, the monastic ideal of "repudiation of all idolatry of the flesh" pervaded the mundane life in those

---

35. 28 M. LUTHER, WORKS 10 (H. Oswald ed. 1972). See also *id.* at 28, where Luther points out that few people have God's grace for chastity and a special gift for it. "For every chaste person there should be more than a hundred thousand married people."
36. *Id.* at 11. See also *id.* at 50: "God will not regard [chaste persons] any more highly than other Christians."
37. *Id.* at 27.
38. See COLE, *supra* note 34, at 118-135.
39. M. WEBER, THE PROTESTANT ETHIC AND THE SPIRIT OF CAPITALISM 95-183 (T. Parsons transl. 1958).
40. *Id.* at 158.

countries in which the Protestant religions formed the basis of the ethical codes.[41]

It cannot be assumed, of course, that the ideal of absolute continence for clerics and the more limited ideal of restraint within the confines of marriage were generally observed in the Christian communities governed by this moral philosophy. It has been pointed out, for example, that in sixteenth-century Europe the vows of celibacy were violated by the clergy on a wide scale.[42] This was, however, a time in which Catholicism went through a severe crisis in many fields of its activities, a crisis which in that very century produced the Prostestant revolt. It is generally assumed that on an overall basis the moral teachings of the Christian churches had an inhibiting effect on sexual freedom.[43] The legal norms against adultery and fornication were frequently enforced; the Church also applied the sanctions available to it, including excommunication, in many cases of violations of the clerical chastity vows. Even in much later times, Sigmund Freud emphasized the repressive effect on the sexual life which the Victorian code of morality had produced in Roman-Catholic Austria, and the situation was not essentially different in the Protestant areas of Europe.

The cultural achievements of the civilization which succeeded that of antiquity were very impressive. In richness, breadth, and diversity, they surpassed the great accomplishments of the Greeks and Romans. Although the most challenging issues of philosophy were already discussed by Plato and Aristotle in a penetrating way, the philosophers of our own civilization, including such names as St. Thomas Aquinas, Duns Scotus, Descartes, Spinoza, Leibniz, Hobbes, Locke, Hume, Kant, Hegel, William James, and Nicolai Hartmann, broadened the scope of philosophical inquiry immensely; they added a great many insights which the more limited historical experience of antiquity had not been able to supply. The art of painting flourished in medieval and postmedieval Europe in a way unparalleled in ancient

---

41. *Id.* at 121, 154, 169.
42. COLE, *supra* note 34, at 111.
43. On the institutionalization of asceticism in medieval Europe see N. CANTOR, MEDIEVAL HISTORY 438-449 (1963).

civilization. The great variety of elaborate architectural styles used in the erection of churches and secular buildings stands in sharp contrast to the relative simplicity and uniformity of classical temples and other edifices. Although we do not know a great deal about the musical accomplishments of the ancient world, there is no question that they did not match the superb productions of a Haydn, Mozart, Bach, Beethoven, Schubert, Brahms, Wagner, and Verdi. The ancient world did produce a few great dramatists, but the size of its literary output remained far behind the rich yield of our own civilization. It can also not be denied that the social sciences in our civilization surpassed in scope, depth, and diversification the attainments of Greece and Rome. As far as the natural sciences and technology are concerned, the width of the gap is too obvious to require elaboration.

Whether the impressive achievements of our civilization may be explained, at least in part, by reference to Freud's and Unwin's thesis is not susceptible to clear verification. If the theory of these authors is accepted, the conclusion will be reached that the energy saved by a restrictive sexual code is apt to be diverted or "sublimated" into cultural effort. One piece of evidence which lends credence to the theory is the fact that the greatest creative minds have usually dedicated their lives more or less exclusively to the pursuits of culture and the human spirit.[44] Scheler has pointed out that genius is characterized by a surplus of spiritual energy over the biological endowment.[45] Alfred Adler has shown that geniuses for the most part had many obstacles to contend with, which stemmed from certain physical handicaps or imperfections.[46] Kretschmer has corroborated these insights in his detailed studies of outstanding personalities.[47]

---

44. This is attested by the biographies of such men as Plato, St. Thomas Aquinas, Spinoza, Kant, Bentham, John Stuart Mill, Beethoven, Brahms, and Tchaikovsky, who lived their lives exclusively or predominantly in an ascetic way.
45. M. SCHELER, DIE WISSENSFORMEN UND DIE GESELLSCHAFT 54 (2d ed. 1960).
46. THE INDIVIDUAL PSYCHOLOGY OF ALFRED ADLER 213 (H.&R. Ansbacher ed. 1956).
47. E. KRETSCHMER, GENIALE MENSCHEN (5th ed. 1958).

While the (total or partial) ascetic dedication of great minds to the tasks of civilization finds its explanation in these facts, the acceptance of a restrictive moral code, involving a substantial sacrifice of highly intense forms of gratification, by large masses of people presents a genuine puzzle. If Freud was right in characterizing the sexual instinct as an imperious tyrant which retaliates against noncompliance with its promptings by various kinds of psychic disturbances, why were millions of people in late antiquity, the Middle Ages, and the postmedieval period willing to put substantial fetters on their natural inclinations? Why, for example, did so many persons in the Roman Empire exchange free-wheeling enjoyment of sex for the austere restrictions of early Christianity? This question has received little attention in the philosophical, sociological, and psychological literature.

Freud himself addressed this question in a few brief passages which have rarely been commented on. He said that "the sexual function has been accompanied by a repugnance which cannot be further accounted for, and which prevents its complete satisfaction and forces it away from the sexual aim into sublimations and libidinal displacements."[48] He added to this statement the hypothesis that what might be involved here was some form of defense of human beings against their earlier animal existence. If this hypothesis is true, one should conclude that cultural activity is not in the first place a sublimation of suppressed libidinal urges; it is a result of the fact that human beings possess an original (i.e., not merely derived) power called "the spirit." The spirit will tend to revolt against an excessive glorification of sex and, by a normal process, withdraw some energy from it for social and cultural purposes.[49] It is relevant in this connection to note the observation of St. Augustine that human beings may (and in his opinion should) prefer a life which pays tribute to the spirit to one directed solely to physical pleasures, because the spirit is

---

48. FREUD, *supra* note 15, at 53.
49. This was the conclusion reached by Max Scheler, who disagreed with Freud's thesis that spiritual energy was nothing but repressed and sublimated sexual energy. M. SCHELER, MAN'S PLACE IN NATURE 54-71 (H. Meyerhoff transl. 1961).

much more obedient to man's free will and purposive direction than the body.[50]

E. SEXUAL MORALITY TODAY AND TOMORROW

Today, the sexual scene in the Western world resembles that which prevailed in the Roman Empire during the first two centuries after the birth of Christ. Since the present permissive approach is a reaction against an era of restriction more severe than that preceding the relaxation of moral norms in Rome, the swing of the pendulum in our time may be more extreme. There are no signs that the present trend will be reversed to a far-reaching extent in the foreseeable future. The drawbacks and possible psychic disturbances portrayed by Freud as consequences of a restrictive code are not imaginary; although the sexual liberation movement has not brought in its train all the benefits envisaged by its protagonists,[51] any return to the philosophy of St. Paul and St. Augustine is out of the question. This conclusion is strengthened by the fact that the fears of illegitimate issue and doubtful paternity, which once militated against an unregulated sexual environment, have been greatly reduced in our times by the invention of effective birth control methods.

It is possible, on the other hand, that there may set in a counterreaction against the more radical manifestations of the sexual revolution. Unwin's thesis that an increase in sexual

---

50. "At times the urge intrudes uninvited; at other times it deserts the panting lover, and although desire is ablaze in the mind, the body is frigid. In this strange fashion lust refuses service not only to the will to procreate but also to the lust for wantonness; and though for the most part it solidly opposes the mind's restraint, there are times when it is divided even against itself and, having aroused the mind, inconsistently fails to arouse the body." ST. AUGUSTINE, THE CITY OF GOD AGAINST THE PAGANS, Bk. XIV. xvi (P. Levine transl. 1966).

51. PACKARD, *supra* note 29, especially Part I; C. LASCH, THE CULT OF NARCISSISM 187-206 (1979). See also B. BETTELHEIM, SURVIVING AND OTHER ESSAYS 370-386 (1979) and Maslow, *Psychological Data and Value Theory,* in NEW KNOWLEDGE OF HUMAN VALUES 133 (A. Maslow ed. 1959).

opportunity is always accompanied by a decrease in mental and material productivity seems to find confirmation in widely-observed reductions in the quality of work and services, especially in the United States and Western Europe.[52] Furthermore, if in marriage an inordinate emphasis is placed on its sexual side, this might have an inhibiting effect on vocational accomplishment by one or both partners; some degree of forbearance is needed when heavy demands are made on the time and energies of a married person. In view of these facts, the forces interested in the preservation of civilization may undertake a major effort to stem a tide which, if carried too far, may endanger the maintenance of civilized forms of life.

It is at this very point that the problem of individual responsibility moves into the limelight. From every conceivable point of view, the benefits of civilization are of such overwhelming value to mankind that a duty toward its preservation and improvement arises in every human being. This means, first of all, that creative activity by self-renouncing devotees of the human spirit should not be discouraged by an anti-intellectual attitude exalting the purely biological values. It means, secondly, that a substantial part of the limited energies of human beings should be reserved for the productive work of civilization-building.[53] If the unthinkable should happen, if large parts of the globe should become devastated by atomic warfare, the need for a renewal of civilization would make even more far-reaching demands on the use of these energies.

It is of little concern whether human contributions to civilization are large or small, manual or mental. The most elevated and imposing accomplishments of culture-growth are made possible only by innumerable small-scale contributions by millions of people who make the wheels of indispensable daily chores, routines, and services go around. What counts is that everyone "must add one stitch, no matter how small it may

---

52. See *supra* Chapter 7 (A) and PACKARD, *supra* note 29, at 309-313, reporting on the early Soviet experience with sexual freedom.

53. It was pointed out earlier that for many human beings the insecurity produced by inconstancy of sexual relations and the ever-present threat of infidelity and termination will have an inhibiting effect on social productivity. See *supra* Chapter 5 (B).

be, to the magnificent tapestry of life."[54] Otherwise our fate is likely to be a return to the dark spectacle of primitive survival.

It is always hazardous to predict the future, but there is a good chance that the next few centuries will witness the advent of a universal order which will eschew the two extremes of ascetic spirituality and hedonistic materialism. This coming age will tend to look with favor on discipline, hard work, and constancy in personal relations without repudiating vitalistic values and the cultivation of the joys of life. It will honor the person who will choose the life of the spirit for the sake of a socially valuable task, but it will pronounce no censure upon the individual who will relish the more earthy pursuits in a morally responsible way. The concept of happiness in such a society will be a polymorphous one; it will allow for the achievement of *eudaimonia*[55] by dedication to spiritual or material values, and to a healthy blending of the two as a general preference.

---

54. P. TEILHARD DE CHARDIN, TOWARDS THE FUTURE 126 (R. Hague transl. 1973).
55. The Greek word *eudaimonia* means inner harmony and wellbeing.

Index of Names

Adler, Alfred, 61, 79n, 131
Aeschylus, 122
Agretelis, D., 31n, 32n
Allen, Francis A., 117n
Allport, Gordon W., 55n, 56n, 62, 66
Andenaes, Johannes, 17n, 36n, 44n
Aquinas, Thomas, 21n, 56, 122, 128, 130, 131n
Arenella, Peter, 47n
Aristotle, 31, 32, 33, 56, 130
Ashley Montague, M., 58n
Augustine, 132, 133

Bach, Johann Sebastian, 131
Barnes, Harry E., 36n
Barnes, Hazel E., 7n, 74
Beauvoir, Simone de, 70, 85n
Beethoven, Ludwig van, 56, 131
Bentham, Jeremy, 100, 131n
Berman, Harold J., 93n
Bettelheim, Bruno, 133n
Blatchford, Robert, 24, 26

Bodenheimer, Brigitte M., 73n, 76n
Bodenheimer, Edgar, 10n, 25n, 33n, 83n, 95n, 110n, 117n
Bohm, David, 19n, 21n
Bohr, Niels, 19n
Born, Max, 19n, 20, 21, 28n
Brahms, Johannes, 131
Branden, Nathaniel, 15n, 16n
Bronfenbrenner, Uri, 76n, 81n
Brown, Norman O., 124, 125n
Buber, Martin, 114
Bunge, Mario, 19n, 20, 21

Calvin, John, 129
Cantor, Norman F., 130n
Cardozo, Benjamin N., 49
Cheng, T.H., 6n, 82n
Cole, W.G., 128n, 129n, 130n
Confucius, 12, 82

Dain, Norman, 35n

137

Davidson, Donald, 23n
Dembitz, Nanette, 81
Descartes, René, 130
Diamond, Bernard L., 35n, 41n
Dix, George E., 48n
Dobzhansky, Theodosius, 27, 124
Dworkin, Ronald, 87n

Edwards, Rem B., 24n
Ehrmann, Henry W., 118n
Einstein, Albert, 2, 19
Eldefonso, Edward, 75n
Euripides, 122
Eycken, Heinrich von, 128n
Eysenck, Hans J., 79n

Farson, Richard E., 77, 83n, 84n
Fearey, Robert, 15, 16n
Feldbrugge, F.J.M., 99n
Fingarette, Herbert, 39n, 44n, 47n, 49n
Fingarette Hasse, A., 39n, 44n, 47n, 49n
Fletcher, George P., 34n, 41n, 47n
Fletcher, Joseph, 90-93
Frankl, Viktor E., ix, 27, 58n, 62, 63n, 65, 115n
Frederick the Great, 116
Freud, Anna, 75n
Freud, Sigmund, 11, 18n, 25, 57, 58n, 61, 69-70, 124-126, 127, 130, 131, 132, 133
Friedlaender, Ludwig, 128n
Fromm, Erich, 24, 56n, 58n, 61, 115n
Fuller, Lon L., 101n

Galsworthy, John, 68
Gandhi, Mahatma, 65
Gerber, R.G., 39n
Glasser, William, 36n, 75n
Glueck, Eleanor, 75n
Glueck, Sheldon, 75n
Goethe, Johann Wolfgang, 63
Goldstein, Abraham S., 41n
Goldstein, Joseph, 75n, 80n
Goode, William J., 76
Gordon, Suzanne, 76n
Green, Robert, 84n
Gregory, Charles O., 99n
Guardini, Romano, 116

Hall, Jerome, 9n, 10n, 33n
Halleck, Seymour L., 25, 37, 41n
Hart, H.L.A., 10n, 23n, 38, 39
Hartmann, Nicolai, 130
Haydn, Joseph, 131
Hazard, Geoffrey, Jr., 45n
Hegel, G.W.F., 130
Heidegger, Martin, 7, 123
Heisenberg, Werner, 19n
Heracleitus, 122
Hirschi, Travis, 75n
Hobbes, Thomas, 12, 57, 87, 130
Holmes, Oliver W., 16
Holt, John C., 83
Honoré, A.M., 23n
Hospers, John, 25
Hume, David, 130

James, William, 130
Jaspers, Karl, 7
Jefferson, Thomas, 116
Jesus, 64
Jolowicz, H.F., 6n, 82n

Index of Names

Kadish, Sanford H., 39n, 41n
Kafka, Franz, 117
Kant, Immanuel, 7, 12, 17, 18n, 27, 28, 92n, 130, 131n
Kaser, Max, 82n
Katz, Sanford N., 80n
Kelly, Joan B., 73n, 75n
Kiefer, Otto, 128n
Klages, Ludwig, 123-124
Kluckhohn, Clyde N., 94n, 95, 121n
Kohlberg, Lawrence, 94n, 95n
Kohler, Joseph, 121
Krause, Harry D., 72n, 80n
Kretschmer, Ernst, 131
Kroeber, A.L., 121n

LaFave, Wayne R., 33n, 42n
Lasch, Christopher, 133n
Lasswell, Harold D., 113
Leibniz, G.W., 130
Levy, Robert J., 80n
Lincoln, Abraham, 116
Linton, Ralph, 94n, 95n
Lippmann, Walter, 108, 110
Locke, John, 12, 130
Loewenstein, Karl, 113
Lorenz, Konrad, 58n
Louisell, David W., 45n
Luther, Martin, 129

MacIver, Robert M., 12, 120
Malinowski, Bronislaw, 58n, 121n
Marcus Aurelius, 116
Maslow, Abraham H., 54, 55n, 56n, 61-62, 133n
Mausbach, Joseph, 128n
Mead, Margaret, 81n, 94n, 95n

Menninger, Karl, 36n
Mill, John Stuart, 12, 16n, 131n
Mises, Richard von, 19n
Mnookin, Robert H., 80n
Mommsen, Theodor, 6n
Monahan, John, 75n
Morgenthau, Hans J., 113, 114
Morris, Herbert, 35n
Morris, Norval, 37
Mosca, Gaetano, 112, 113n
Mozart, Wolfgang A., 131
Murray, John E., 103n

Napoleon, 115
Newton, Isaac, 2, 18
Nietzsche, Friedrich, 113, 115-116, 123
Northrop, F.S.C., 21
Nowell-Smith, P.H., 15n
Nye, Francis I., 75n

Packard, Vance, 127n, 133n, 134n
Pareto, Vilfredo, 113
Paul (Apostle), 91, 92, 128, 133
Pericles, 116
Planck, Max, 19n
Plato, 31, 112, 122, 130, 131n
Prosser, William L., 99n, 100n

Radbruch, Gustav, 121
Rand, Ayn, 64-65
Rée, Paul, 17n
Reel, A. Frank, 118n
Reisner, Ralph, 39n
Richards, David A.J., 98n

Ringer, Robert R., 65n
Róheim, Géza, 124
Russell, Bertrand, 19n, 114

Sartre, Jean-Paul, 7, 88, 89, 90
Scheler, Max, 131, 132n
Schilder, Paul, 56n
Schlick, Moritz, 15n
Schoenfeld, C.G., 35n
Schopenhauer, Arthur, 18, 26, 27
Schubert, Franz, 131
Schulz, Fritz, 104n
Schweitzer, Albert, 70
Scott, Austin, 33n
Scotus, Duns, 130
Seligman, Martin E.P., 36n
Semmel, Herbert, 39n
Shakespeare, William, 124n
Shuman, Samuel I., 58-60, 77n
Smith, Adam, 106
Smith, T.V., 12n
Socrates, 64
Solnit, Albert J., 75n
Sophocles, 122
Sorokin, Pitirim, 127
Spengler, Oswald, 120
Spinoza, Benedict, 130, 131n
Stirner, Max, 10, 11, 63, 70, 87
Szasz, Thomas S., 34, 35, 37

Tammelo, Ilmar, 116n
Tchaikovsky, Peter I., 131n

Teeters, N.K., 36n
Teilhard de Chardin, Pierre, 135n
Thrasymachus, 112
Toynbee, Arnold, 127
Tylor, Edward B., 121n

Unger, Roberto M., 63
Unwin, Joseph D., 126-127, 131, 133

Verdi, Giuseppe, 131

Waelder, Robert, 41n
Wagner, Richard, 131
Wald, Michael, 80n
Wallerstein, Judith S., 73n, 75n
Warnock, Mary, 7n
Weber, Max, 129
Wechsler, Herbert, 43n
Weiss, Paul, 23n
Wertham, Frederic, 36n
Whitehead, Alfred N., 79n
Wild, John, 7n
Wolff, Hans J., 104n
Wootton, Barbara, 38, 39

Zilboorg, Gregory, 36n

Index of Subjects

Act of God, 8, 9-10. *See also* Chance
Adultery, 89, 98, 130
Aggression, impulse of, 57-58, 75, 124
Alcoholism, 58, 60, 76, 81. *See also* Intoxication
Alimony. *See* Support obligations, legal
Altruism, 63-66, 92
Analects, 12. *See also* Confucius
Asceticism, 127-130, 131 n. 44, 132, 135
Authority, parental, 77-79, 82-83, 84
Autonomy:
  moral, 88, 89-90, 93;
  parental, 79, 80-82

Birth control, 133
Blameworthiness, 9, 14, 31, 38, 40, 118. *See also Mens rea*
Bureaucracy, 104, 117

Categorical imperative, 12, 53
Catholic Church, 72, 128, 130
Causality, 2, 14-15, 17-23, 28. *See also* Quantum theory; Physics
  individual, 20-22, 23
  law-governed, 17-18, 19-21
Celibacy. *See* Asceticism
Censors (Roman), 5-7
Chance, 19. *See also* Act of God
Character (of individuals), 26-27
Child abuse, 79, 80
Child neglect, 6, 75, 76, 79-80, 81-82
Children, responsibility toward, 1, 73, 74-82, 99. *See also* Education
Children's Rights, 77, 83-84, 105
China, 82, 94
Choice. *See* Freewill
Christianity, 7, 91, 99, 128, 129-130, 132. *See also*

141

Christianity *(cont.)*
  Catholic Church; Protestantism; Religion
Civilization, 8, 13, 104, 120-123, 124-126, 126-127, 132, 134
  ancient, 122-123, 127-128, 130
  Judaeo-Christian, 7, 127-132
  medieval, 98, 128, 130-131, 132
  skeptical views on, 123-124, 126
Common good. *See* Welfare, public
Conflict, social, 1, 87, 65-66, 106-107, 112, 115
Conscience, 7
Contracts, 94, 95, 102-103
Corporations, 103, 104, 106, 117
Corruption, 1, 6, 36
Crime, 1, 28, 33, 59, 60, 88-89, 93-94, 98. *See also* Juvenile Delinquency; Punishment
Criminal law, 28, 33-49, 78, 99, 117
Criminology, 2
Culpability. *See* Blameworthiness; *Mens rea*
Culture. *See* Civilization

Damages, 5, 8-9. *See also* Torts
Delinquency. *See* Crime; Juvenile Delinquency
Democracy, 108-109, 110, 122
Determinism, 1-2, 14-19, 21,

Determinism *(cont.)*
  27-28, 40, 44
Dhammapada, 12
Diminished responsibility. *See* Responsibility, diminished
Divorce, 6, 72-74, 75
Drugs, 58, 60, 81, 89, 93
Duress, 32, 33

Education, 1, 6, 66, 77, 78-79, 80, 83-84, 86, 101, 105, 107, 111, 116. *See also* Children's rights; Sex education
Egotism, 1, 10, 11, 63-66, 87, 89. *See also* Special interests
Environment:
  as affecting character, 15-16, 26-27
  protection of, 1, 106
Equality, 111, 115
Ethics, 6, 8, 11-13, 14, 78, 96-97, 115. *See also* Golden Rule; Responsibility, moral; Situation ethics
  relativism in, 91-93
  universal principles of, 78, 94-96
Existentialism, 7-8, 74

Family, responsibilities of members, 72-85
Fault. *See* Blameworthiness; *Mens Rea*
France, 115, 118n
Fraud, 94, 95
Freedom, 110-111, 115. *See*

Index of Subjects

Freedom *(cont.)*
 also Sexual freedom
Freewill, 2, 9, 14-29, 30, 40, 44, 49

Genius, 131
Golden Rule, 11-12, 74, 85, 86n
Greek culture. *See* Civilization, ancient

Health, 58-60, 75, 77, 79, 80, 81, 86, 93, 106, 107, 111
Hedonism, 10, 62, 65, 70, 73, 76, 89, 125, 128, 132, 133
Heredity, 15-16, 26-27
Homicide, 32, 33, 35, 45-48, 88-89, 91, 92, 94, 95-96
Homosexuality, 98
Human nature. *See* Nature, human

Idealism, 61-62, 114-115
Ignorance:
 of facts, 31, 32, 33
 of law, 33, 78
Incest, 77, 94, 95
Insanity, 34-45
 abolition of defense, 37-41
 definition of, 37, 41
 irrestible impulse test, 42, 43
 M'Naghten test, 41-42, 43, 48
 Model Penal Code test, 42-45, 48
Instincts, 11, 54-56, 123, 124, 125, 126, 127

Interest groups. *See* Special interests
Intoxication, as a legal defense, 47. *See also* Alcoholism
Involuntary acts, 31-32. *See also* Determinism; Duress
Irresistible impulse. *See* Insanity, irresistible impulse test

Japan, 82, 94
Judaism, 7
Juvenile delinquency, 75, 93-94

Knowledge, quest for, 56-57, 111

Labor organizations, 106, 107
Laws. *See also* Criminal law; Natural law; Roman law; Torts
 physical, 17-18, 20, 21, 23
 statistical, 19, 95
Lawyers, 103, 104
Legal Responsibility, 2, 5, 8, 34, 35, 38, 44, 48, 70-71, 97-101, 111
Liability, strict. *See* Strict liability
Love, 28, 55-56, 68-70, 91-93, 97

Mahabharata, 12
Marital partners, responsibil-

Marital partners *(cont.)*
ity toward, 72-74
Marriage, 72-74, 128, 129, 130, 134. *See also* Monogamy; Polygamy
Marxism, 122
Mens rea, 32-33, 37, 38, 39, 40. *See also* Voluntary acts
Mental disorder, 2, 36, 45. *See also* Insanity
Metaphysics, 12
Middle Ages. *See* Catholic Church; Civilization, medieval
Model Penal Code. *See* Insanity, Model Penal Code test
Monogamy, 70, 73, 126-127, 128. *See also* Marriage
Moral Responsibility, 2, 5-7, 8, 9, 14-15, 38, 67-71, 86-101, 107. *See also* Ethics
Morality. *See* Ethics; Moral responsibility
Motives, battle of, 23-26, 28. *See also* Unconscious motivation
Murder. *See* Homicide

Natural law, 95
Nature, human, 11, 54-57, 63, 74, 95, 96
Necessity, as a legal defense, 33
Needs, human, 54-57. *See also* Sexuality, human
Negligence, 9, 32-33, 117, 118
New Testament, 11, 91, 92, 128. *See also* Golden Rule

Old age, 84-85
Old Testament, 82, 88-89, 98, 128. *See also* Ten Commandments

Parental authority. *See* Authority, parental
Parental autonomy. *See* Autonomy parental
Parents, responsibility toward, 82-85
in ancient Rome, 6, 82-83
in China and Japan, 82
Perjury, 89
Permissiveness, 77-78
Physics, 2, 18-21
Polygamy, 111
Pornography, 77-78
Power impulse, 55, 89, 108, 112-114, 115-116
Property, 94, 96, 111, 112
Protestantism, 129-130
Psychoanalysis, 123-124, 124-126, 130, 132. *See also* Freud, Sigmund; Sublimation of instinct
Punishment, 5, 8, 15-17, 30-31, 35, 36-37. *See also* Crime; Criminal law
Puritanism, 129-130. *See also* Asceticism

Quantum theory, 19, 21. *See also* Physics

Rationality. *See* Reason
Reality principle (Freud), 11

Index of Subjects

Reason:
  as a brake on impulse, 11, 12, 28, 29, 43, 44
  as a human endowment, 7, 18, 57, 123
  distinguished from cause, 22-23
Recognition, quest for, 55
Religion, 7, 12, 65, 72, 91, 92, 96, 98, 99, 121, 127, 128-130, 131
Rescue, duty to, 99-100
Respect, duty to show, 12, 74, 85, 87, 92
Responsibility. See also Children, responsibility toward; Legal responsibility; Marital partners, responsibility toward; Moral Responsibility; Parents, responsibility toward; Sexual partners, responsibility toward
  anonymity of, 117-119
  causal, 9-10
  concept of, 5-9
  diminished, 45-48
  existential, 7, 8, 9, 11, 53-63, 66, 93, 101
  limits of, 25-26, 30-49
  political, 1, 8, 107-110, 114-116
  roots of, 10-13
  social, 1, 2, 8, 9, 102-107
  transpersonal, 2, 13, 107, 120-135
Rights, human, 1, 110-112, 115. See also Children's rights
Roman culture. See Civilization, ancient
Roman law, 5-7, 82-83, 104
Ruling class, 112-113, 115-116. See also Power impulse

Safety, desire for, 11, 16, 55. See also Security
Sanctions, 6, 8-9
  legal, 5, 6, 8-9, 30, 98, 99
  social, 6, 8-9
Security, 55, 111, 115. See also Safety, desire for; Stability in family life
Self-actualization, 7-8, 53, 61, 62-63, 87, 102, 111. See also Self-perfection
Self-defense:
  collective, 16
  individual, 33, 88
Self-determination, 27
Self-perfection, 11, 26, 60-63, 66. See also Self-actualization
Selfishness. See Egotism; Special interests
Sex education, 77-78
Sexual freedom, 127, 128, 130, 132, 133-134
  of children, 77-78
Sexual partners, responsibility toward, 67-71
Sexuality, human, 54, 55, 70, 124-125, 127, 132, 133. See also Homosexuality
Situation ethics, 78, 90-94, 97. See also Ethics
Special interests, 1, 106, 107, 112, 117-118
Spirit, human, 13, 18, 123, 124, 131, 132-133, 134,

Spirit *(cont.)*
    135
Stability in family life, 73-74, 75, 76
Strict liability, 9-10, 38-39
Sublimation of instinct, 125, 131, 132. *See also* Freud, Sigmund; Psychoanalysis
Suicide, 76
Support obligations, legal, 72-73

Ten Commandments, 82, 88, 98. *See also* Old Testament
Theft, 89, 94, 96
Torts, 78, 94, 95, 98, 99-100, 105

Unconscious motivation, 25-
Unconscious motivation *(cont.)* 26
Unfair competition, 98

Values, human, 88, 90, 91, 92-93, 97, 120-121, 135. *See also* Ethics; Spirit, human
    biological, 123-124, 131, 132-133, 134, 135
    conflicts between, 96-97
    universal, 94-96, 97
Voluntary acts, 31-33, 36. *See also Mens rea*

War, 87, 89, 96-97, 116, 118, 119, 134
Welfare, public, 16, 106-107, 110, 112, 113, 116
West Germany, criminal code of, 33 n. 12 & 13, 48

Table of Cases

Durham v. United States, 41n

Hurley v. Eddingfield, 100n

Marvin v. Marvin, 68n, 71
McDonald v. United States, 41n
M'Naghten's Case, 42, 43, 48

O'Keefe v. W.J. Barry Co., 100n
Orr v. Orr, 72n

People v. Conley, 46n, 47
People v. Drew, 43n, 48n
People v. Goedecke, 46n
People v. Gorshen, 46

People v. Poddar, 46n
People v. Wells, 45-46
Peter W. v. San Francisco Unified School District, 105n

Rex v. Byrne, 45n

State v. Strasburg, 40
Steward Machine Company v. Davis, 49

United States v. Brawner, 37n, 41n
United States v. Currens, 42n

Zelenko v. Gimbel Bros., 100n